# MICRONATIONS

Invent Your Own Country and Culture

with **25** Projects

The Commonwealth of Beachland

**Kathy Ceceri**
Illustrated by Chad Thompson

## ~ Latest titles in the *Build It Yourself* Series ~

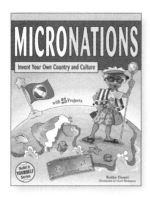
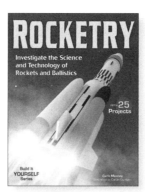

Check out more titles at www.nomadpress.net

Nomad Press
A division of Nomad Communications
10 9 8 7 6 5 4 3 2 1

This book was manufactured by Sheridan Books, Ann Arbor, MI USA.
May 2014, Job #358382
ISBN: 978-1-61930-218-1

Illustrations by Chad Thompson
Educational Consultant, Marla Conn

Questions regarding the ordering of this book should be addressed to
Nomad Press
2456 Christian St.
White River Junction, VT 05001
www.nomadpress.net

# CONTENTS

**I would like to thank the following people
for their help with this book:**

Beau Breslin, Ph.D., of Skidmore College

His Excellency Kevin Baugh, President of Molossia

King James III (Jamie Sheffield) of the Northern Forest Archipelago

His Imperial Majesty Doctor Eric Lis of the Aerican Empire

## Create Your Own Micronation

**HAVE YOU EVER WONDERED WHAT IT WOULD BE LIKE** to invent your own **country**? That's what **micronations** are all about! A micronation is an imaginary country that has many things real countries have. Most micronations have a leader, a **government**, and laws. Some also have a flag, stamps, and money, as well as their own music, language, and holidays.

### WORDS TO KNOW!

**country:** a place with official boundaries, called borders, that mark it off from other places. A country can make agreements or fight wars with other countries.

**micronation:** an imaginary country that has many features of a real country, but is not considered real by other countries.

**government:** an organization or system that controls a city, state, or country.

## WORDS TO KNOW!

**citizen:** a person who legally belongs to a country and has the rights and protection of that country.

**nation:** another word for country, also used to refer to a group of people who share a common culture even if they don't live in their own country.

**culture:** the beliefs and way of life of a group of people, which can include religion, language, art, clothing, food, holidays, and more.

**tradition:** a custom or belief that has been handed down in a community or culture over many years.

*The main difference between a micronation and a real country is whether other countries in the world agree that it is real.*

Micronations have been created by kids and by adults. They can be found in forests, in deserts, and on platforms in the middle of the ocean. Some are no bigger than a back yard or a bedroom. A few allow visitors, but most micronations are only open to their own **citizens**. And many exist only online, where they can be seen by anyone.

This book will take you through the steps of creating your own micronation. You'll be given great power—but with it comes great responsibility. Besides getting to call yourself "Lord Blake III, Ruler of Dragoria, Duke of Coventry" or "Queen Sofia of Quy Quorta," you can bestow titles on your friends and give them the top jobs in your government.

As the founder of your **nation**, you can choose what kind of systems and laws will help your country achieve its goals. And you get to name holidays, establish a **culture** with **traditions**, and even invent a language that will bind your people together.

Activities and projects in this book will show you how to create **artifacts** that make your micronation seem real. **You will learn to:**

- Write your own **declaration of independence** explaining what your new country is about;

- Make a **map** of your territory, including famous **landmarks** and historical monuments;

- Design a flag that symbolizes your country's ideals;

- Put together an **atlas** of facts and figures about micronations; and

- Organize a Micronational World's Fair where you can share your country's culture and traditions with others.

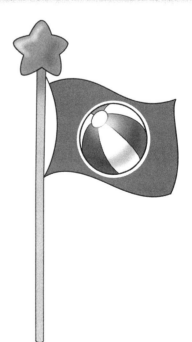

3

As you discover more about micronations, you will also learn about **geography**. First, you'll look at **physical geography**, which deals with the shape of the land, as well as the water, weather, and living things there. You'll also explore **cultural geography**, which focuses on people and the way they interact with the physical geography around them. And you will practice **world-building** to invent a made-up place that seems real.

*So welcome to the world of micronations! It's your chance to be in charge—and find out what makes a country a country!*

## WORDS TO KNOW!

**geography:** the study of the earth and its features, such as mountains and rivers, and the effect of human activity on the earth.

**physical geography:** the land, water, and weather in an area.

**cultural geography:** the way people interact with their surroundings. Also called human geography.

**world-building:** the process of inventing an imaginary world in a book, movie, or game.

**characteristic:** a feature of a person, place, or thing.

**theme:** a central, recurring idea or concept.

**liberty:** freedom, the ability to act or live freely as one chooses.

## Find a Theme for Your Country

What is the most important **characteristic** of your country? What is the main idea behind it? Coming up with a **theme** is useful when designing a micronation.

For instance, the theme of the United States of America is **liberty**, or freedom. This is a very important idea to Americans, and it shows up in the country's songs, documents, and symbols. The Declaration of Independence says that everyone has the right to "life, liberty, and the pursuit of happiness."

The United States **Constitution** includes the **Bill of Rights**, which guarantees certain freedoms to the country's citizens. These include freedom of speech, **freedom of the press**, and **freedom of religion**.

## World-Building in Books and Games

Science fiction and fantasy writers use world-building to create a fictional setting where their characters live. Many of the countries in books and stories are as richly detailed as any micronation. When J.R.R. Tolkien created Middle Earth, the setting for *The Lord of the Rings* and *The Hobbit*, he drew maps of its landscape and invented a language written and spoken only by elves. In the *Harry Potter* series, author J.K. Rowling created a magical world for wizards and witches that exists in and around the places where ordinary Muggles live. Harry's world has its own schools, such as Hogwarts, its own sports, such as Quidditch, and even its own favorite snacks, such as chocolate frogs and butter beer.

Video games such as *Minecraft*, *The Sims*, and *Second Life* give players a chance to create their own settings and characters using materials they find in the game or make themselves. Players can invite friends to come "visit" the worlds they create without ever leaving home!

As you work on your own micronation, keep your country's theme in mind. Everything about your invented country can relate to your theme. An example is a micronation called Aqualand. Created by a group of fifth-graders as a class project, the most important characteristic of Aqualand was that it was underwater. Its **motto** was "Bubbles, Bubbles, and More Bubbles," and its national animal was the fish. The micronation of Backyardistan, founded in 2012 near Hollywood, California, features a garden hose on its **coat of arms** and a lawn chair surrounded by barbecue grills on its flag.

Remember, you can make your micronation as simple or as fancy as you like. This country is just for you!

*The most important thing is to make your country the kind of place where you'd like to live.*

## WORDS TO KNOW!

**motto:** a saying that represents the main belief or purpose of a person, group, or country.

**coat of arms:** a design made of several symbols that represents a family or country.

**mythology:** a collection of traditional stories, either truthful or overly elaborated, that are often focused on historical events. Myths express the beliefs and values of a group of people.

## National Symbols

A country's symbols usually relate to its theme. They can be based on a nation's history, **mythology**, religion, or even its environment or physical surroundings. What are some national symbols from real countries?

**Animal:** The bald eagle symbolizes strength and determination for the United States. The mythical dragon represents good luck in China. People from New Zealand are called "Kiwis" after a small bird there.

**Flower, Tree, or Plant:** Canada's symbol is the maple leaf, because of the maple trees that grow there. The lotus flower, which stands for purity, is the national symbol of India. The shamrock, or three-leaf clover, is a well-known symbol for Ireland. The flag of Guam, an island in the Pacific, has a palm tree. The cedar tree has been the symbol of Lebanon in the Middle East for thousands of years.

**Color:** The colors red, white, and blue are closely tied to the United States, although they are used by many other countries as well. Green can represent the earth and is associated with Ireland, which is why many people wear green on St. Patrick's Day. In many countries, red symbolizes courage and the blood spilled in war, but it is popular in China as a sign of luck. Many African flags contain the colors red, green, yellow, and sometimes black. Yellow symbolizes the sun, or **wealth**. The color of the **United Nations (UN)** flag and the helmets worn by UN **military** forces is sky blue. Blue often represents freedom and peace.

## WORDS TO KNOW!

**wealth:** money and valuable belongings.

**United Nations (UN):** an organization of countries started in 1945 to encourage peace and improve living conditions around the world. It is based in New York City. Today the UN has 193 member countries.

**military:** the army, navy, air force, and other armed services that protect a country and fight in wars.

**Motto:** The first motto of the United States was *E Pluribus Unum*, which is Latin for "one from many parts." It referred to the country's original 13 **colonies**. France's motto, "Liberty, Equality, **Fraternity**," goes back to the French **Revolution**, when the citizens threw out the king and established their own government.

**Shape:** The five-pointed star is a symbol used by the U.S. military, as well as on the American flag. In Israel, the flag has a six-pointed star, which stands for Judaism. The Australian flag uses a seven-pointed star. A crescent moon is used as a symbol by many Islamic countries, such as Turkey and Pakistan. The Maltese Cross, which has double points on each end, is a medieval symbol still used to represent the country of Malta. The flag of Japan is a large red circle on a white background, symbolizing the sun.

## What's in a Name?

Countries get their names in different ways. They can be named after physical features, the people who live there, or a ruler. Consider the explanations behind the names of the following countries—you may get some ideas for naming your micronation.

Iceland is a small icy island nation near the North Pole. But its neighbor Greenland is also icy. Greenland was named by Erik the Red. He moved there after being banned from Iceland for murder, and hoped the name would attract more Icelanders to join him.

America is named after Italian explorer Amerigo Vespucci. Christopher Columbus became famous in Europe when he sailed to some islands near what is now North and South America. But Vespucci was the first to realize the land was not part of Asia but a whole "New World." A mapmaker who read Vespucci's writing put the name America on a map and it stuck—even after the mapmaker changed his mind.

Bolivia was named after Simon Bolivar, a leader in the war to free South America from control by Spain. Venezuela, also in South America, got its name because of its homes on stilts, which reminded Spanish explorers of the city of Venice in Italy.

## WORDS TO KNOW!

**continent:** one of the earth's large landmasses, including Africa, Antarctica, Australia, North America, South America, and Asia and Europe (called Eurasia).

*South Africa's name reflects its position at the southern tip of the African* **continent**.

Ivory Coast, also in Africa, was once a famous source of ivory. This is a white material used in jewelry and for piano keys that comes from the tusks of elephants. Congo comes from the word used by native Bantu people for "mountain."

## FASCINATING FACT

The oldest country in the world that still exists today is Japan. It was formed more than 2,600 years ago.

Australia comes from the Latin word for "southern" because it is on the southern part of the globe. But nearby New Zealand was named after an island in the northern European country of Denmark.

Singapore's people are mostly of Chinese background. But the country's name is from the ancient Indian language of Sanskrit, meaning "city of lions."

# MAKE YOUR OWN
## Micronation Worksheet

A worksheet will help you organize information about your country. You can just write some general descriptions now. Hold onto it, because you will be using it later and adding more details as you go through the book.

**1** On the paper or computer, make two columns. In one column, you will list categories. In the other, you will add the information for your particular micronation.

**2** Pick a name in keeping with your country's theme. If you need help coming up with a theme, take a piece of paper and brainstorm some ideas. You can do some research by flipping through this book and reading about other micronations and real countries. Then make a list of some things that are important or interesting to you. Look for connections between them. If you can fit most of them into one category, use that as your theme.

**3** Write a brief description of your country. It can just be one or two lines—you'll be coming up with more details in later chapters.

**4** What type of government do you want to be? Give yourself a title. You can make yourself **royal** or give yourself a **political** position. If you need some ideas, take a look at the chart of country and leader names on the next page.

**5** Make up some symbols to go with your country's theme. There are some suggested categories in the sample chart shown here. You can also make up your own. List the ones that apply on your worksheet and fill in the information for your micronation.

### SUPPLIES

- ♂ paper and pencil or computer for writing up lists
- ♂ markers for drawing a design

### W♂RDS T♂ KN♂W!

**royal:** having to do with a king or queen.

**political:** relating to running a government and holding onto power.

| Category | Your Micronation |
|---|---|
| Animal | |
| Flower, Tree, or Plant | |
| Motto | |
| Colors | |
| Shapes | |
| Natural Landmark | |
| Famous Building | |

| Type of Country | Description | Leader |
|---|---|---|
| **Republic** | a government run by its citizens, who get to choose their own leaders. | president or prime minister |
| **Kingdom** | a country run by a king or queen in which power is usually passed down from parent to child or other family member. | king/queen |
| **Commonwealth** | a republic that is an organization of countries, such as the British Commonwealth. | prime minister |
| **State** | another word for a country that can also refer to a small part of a larger country. | |
| **Principality** | a small area or country that is ruled by a prince. | prince/princess |
| **Empire** | a large group of countries or regions controlled by one ruler or government. | emperor/ empress, caesar, czar, kaiser |
| **Federation** | a group of separate states or countries that gives some powers to a central government and keeps some control over local matters. | |

Other types of small countries and their leaders include: duchy (duke or duchess), bailiwick (bailiff), fiefdom (lord or lady), palatinate (palatine), emirate (emir), and sultanate (sultan).

# DESIGN YOUR OWN
## Official Seal

Now that you have some ideas for symbols for your country, use them to create your micronation's official coat of arms

## SUPPLIES

- ☉ paper and pencil
- ☉ marker
- ☉ craft foam
- ☉ scissors
- ☉ glue
- ☉ pieces of cardboard, a flip flop, or blocks of wood small enough to hold
- ☉ inkpad, or paint on a disposable plate

and a **seal**. Seals were originally designs pressed into a soft piece of wax with a mold. A seal put on a document shows that a person or government official has approved it.

## WORDS TO KNOW!

**seal:** an official symbol that shows that a document or other object belongs to the government.

Today, seals are usually stamped on with an inkpad or pressed into a piece of paper with a special tool so that it leaves a raised mark. This project makes a rubbery stamp for putting an inked seal on important documents.

**1** Start by sketching out your micronation's coat of arms. First draw the outside border of your design. Make it thick like the frame on a painting. It can be a circle, a shield, or any shape you like. Then choose some of your micronation's symbols and arrange them inside the border. Keep the symbols simple, and make sure they don't touch each other or the outside border.

**2** To make the stamp, copy your coat of arms onto a sheet of craft foam. To make the backing, take your cardboard, foam backing from a flip-flop shoe, or wood, and lay it on the table with the stamping side facing up.

**3** Cut around the outside shape of your craft foam seal. Turn it over so the drawing on it is facing down. You do that because your stamp must be a mirror image of the final version. Place it on the backing, then trace around it to show where it will go.

12

BUILD IT YOURSELF

**4** Carefully cut out the symbols of your seal from the craft foam. Glue the outside shape onto the backing, again making sure that the side with the drawing is face down onto the backing. Then glue the symbols inside, also facing down.

**5** When it's dry, test your seal with a sheet of scrap paper before you put it on any important documents. Press it onto an inkpad or into a very small amount of paint poured onto a disposable plate. Then press it onto the scrap paper to see how it looks. If you want your seal to appear in different colors, you can carefully brush a thin coat of paint onto just one section or symbol at a time using the colors you would like for your coat of arms. You can also try swirling a few colors around on the plate, keeping them separate, for a multicolor effect.

**6** Find a picture of the Great Seal of the United States. Does your seal have any similarities to the Great Seal? What's different about it? Find images of other official seals and compare your seal to those. What does your seal say about your micronation?

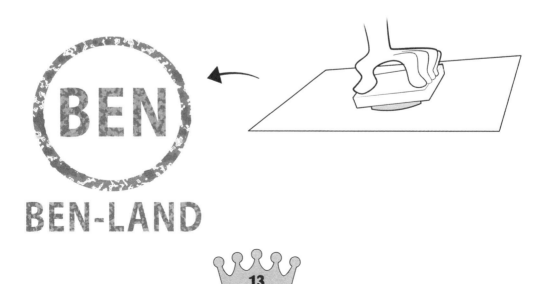

BEN-LAND

# CHAPTER ONE

# What Makes a Country a Country?

**REAL COUNTRIES ARE BEING FORMED**
(and dissolved) all the time. So why aren't
micronations considered real? What are
the rules—and who made them?

# Recognize Me?

The standard definition of a state or country under international law comes from a document called the Montevideo Convention on the Rights and Duties of States. This agreement was signed in 1933 by the United States and other countries from North and South America. **It lists four requirements for a place to be considered a country:**

1. It must have permanent **residents** who want to be citizens of the country;

2. It must have clear borders that separate it from the rest of the world;

3. It must have a government to run things; and

4. It must have the ability to make **treaties** with other governments.

One thing the Montevideo Convention doesn't say is that other countries must **recognize** a new country for it to be considered official. Through the years, a number of micronations have tried to use this **loophole** to declare themselves real. Another definition that is sometimes used, however, says the opposite: The only thing a real country needs is for other countries to recognize it as real.

*Some micronations have claimed recognition by other countries because their* **passports** *were accepted as proof of* **identity** *at a border crossing.*

## WORDS TO KNOW!

**resident:** a person who lives in a place permanently or for a long time.

**treaty:** a written agreement between two countries.

**recognize:** to officially accept something as being true.

**loophole:** a mistake or unclear wording in a law that people use to avoid following the law exactly.

**passport:** a document from the government that identifies a person as a citizen of the country.

**identity:** the unique characteristics of a person, country, or group.

Membership in the United Nations is sometimes considered proof of **statehood**. But the UN itself doesn't recognize countries. Member countries simply vote on whether a new country is allowed to join. The only requirement is that new members must agree to abide by the rules of the UN.

No matter what definition is used, there are a few other things a country must have in order to run smoothly. **They include:**

- An organized **economy** that lets people, companies, and the government exchange **goods** and **services**;

- Systems to provide things such as fire and police protection, a military, education, and health care; and

- **Infrastructure**, including **transportation** (highways, railroads, airports), power (electrical grid, natural gas pipelines), and means of **communication** (postal service, telephone lines, **satellites**).

## WORDS TO KNOW!

**statehood:** the existence of an independent state or country.

**economy:** the system of making and exchanging things of **value**.

**value:** how much money something is worth.

**goods:** things that are made or grown.

**services:** jobs and businesses that provide something for other people but do not produce goods.

**infrastructure:** roads, bridges, and other basic types of structures and equipment needed for a country to function properly.

**transportation:** methods of travel.

**communication:** methods of sending information.

**satellite:** a spacecraft that permanently circles the earth high above its surface to send and receive TV, cell phone, and other communications signals.

Beachland Transportation

*Countries also usually have a culture that is shared by its people—things such as language, customs, traditions, and beliefs.*

There can be different cultures in one country, but the country will function best if they **co-exist** peacefully. When people from different cultures don't get along, there can be arguments and fighting that sometimes leads to **civil war**—and possibly the creation of even more countries.

# Independence Day

Throughout history, new countries have been formed by people who discovered new territory, who wanted to control the area where they lived, or who decided to change the way things were run. Since just about every piece of land has already been discovered, today new countries usually form when one government takes over from another. Sometimes both sides agree, but often it involves **conflict**. **There are generally four ways this can happen.**

**WORDS TO KNOW!**

**co-exist:** to live in peace with each other.

**civil war:** a war between groups of people in the same country.

**conflict:** a long period of disagreement that sometimes includes violence.

**secede:** to break away from a country.

**Secession:** Following a civil war that lasted for decades, the people of Sudan voted to allow South Sudan to **secede** in 2011. Since then, the Republic of South Sudan has struggled to stand on its own, but the world's newest country remains independent.

**Independence granted to former colonies or territories:** After World War II, the United States took control of the Caroline Islands in the Pacific Ocean near Australia. In 1986, the United States granted independence to the islands, which formed a new country known as the Federated States of Micronesia.

**Bigger countries dissolving:** When the Soviet Union broke up in 1991, it divided into 15 newly independent countries, including Russia and Ukraine.

**Joining together with other countries or areas:** After World War II, Germany was divided into two countries. East Germany and West Germany were separated by the Berlin Wall. In 1990, the wall was torn down and the countries merged to again form one country, which we now know as Germany.

## FASCINATING FACT

American video game developer Richard Garriott (also known as Lord British) found some new land to call his own—on the moon. Garriott, the son of an astronaut, spent $68,000 to buy a remote-control buggy that was lost on the moon by the former Soviet Union in 1973. When NASA photos located the missing buggy in 2010, Garriott claimed rights to the property around it. He hopes a private space mission will someday let him visit his personal parking lot on the moon.

## Birth of a Micronation

As with real countries, people create micronations for different reasons—some serious and some not so serious.

Small regions that at one point in history were considered independent are sometimes labeled as micronations today. The Free Republic of Le Saugeais in a mountainous part of France goes back to 1150, when it was established under the protection of a duke. A local innkeeper, Georges Pourchet, was jokingly appointed president by a French official in 1947. The current president is his daughter, Georgette Bertin-Pourchet, who carries on the tradition of helping to promote Le Saugeais to tourists.

Welcome to

**The Republic of Le Saugeais**

## Real Small Countries

Real countries that are very small in land or **population** are sometimes called **microstates**. They include the Principality of Monaco near the border of France and Italy. Ruled by the House of Grimaldi since 1419, its current chief of state is Prince Albert II, son of American movie star Grace Kelly. Nauru, an island in the Pacific, broke away from Australia to become the world's smallest independent republic in 1968.

Some micronations declare their independence as a protest against the government. In 1982, the city of Key West, Florida, broke away from the United States to form a micronation they called the Conch Republic.

The people of Key West were mad because the border police set up a roadblock on the only highway connecting their island to the mainland. The roadblock was meant to catch foreigners trying to sneak into the country, but it also kept tourists from visiting. In protest, the mayor and city council announced that they would secede from the United States.

*After one full minute of independence, the rebels surrendered to U.S. authorities.*

### WORDS TO KNOW!

**population:** the number of people living in a place.

**microstate:** a real nation that is extremely small.

**currency:** money.

### FASCINATING FACT

Seborga might be the oldest micronation in existence. This tiny Italian village has had its own ruler since the time of the Holy Roman Empire, more than a thousand years ago. The current leader is Prince Giorgio I. Seborga still issues its own stamps and **currency**, but otherwise is considered part of Italy.

Some micronations want to be treated like real countries. Sealand may be the only micronation to have fought and won real battles against foreign governments in court—and on the high seas. In the 1960s, Englishman Roy Bates claimed an abandoned World War II defense platform in the middle of the North Sea and declared himself Prince Roy. Bates and his son, Prince Michael, were arrested in 1968 for firing upon a British navy ship sent to remove them. A British judge ruled that Sealand was outside British authority. In 1978, Bates and his son captured a group trying to take over Sealand and held them prisoner. German **diplomats** had to travel to Sealand to arrange their release. Bates died in 2012, leaving Prince Michael in charge.

Many micronations are created as a hobby. The Northern Forest **Archipelago** (NFA) was a "land-based nation-state" founded by Jamie Sheffield, also known as King James II, in the heart of the Adirondack Mountains in upstate New York. As a middle school teacher, Sheffield was curious about how countries work and decided to create his own. For several years he built up the NFA with friends and family. Citizens built a treehouse in his back yard to serve as its **capital**. He printed up NFA stamps, made wooden NFA coins, and created unique systems to run his country.

> # W**O**RDS T**O** KN**O**W!
>
> **diplomat:** a person sent by the government to deal with another country.
>
> **archipelago:** a group of islands, usually arranged in a line near a bigger piece of land.
>
> **capital:** the city where the government of a state or country is based.

Most micronations are created for fun. In 2005, British comedian Danny Wallace hosted a BBC television show called *How to Start Your Own Country*. He founded his country of Lovely in his London apartment. Wallace drew up a declaration of independence, had a flag and a uniform designed, and wrote a **national anthem**. Many fans signed up to become citizens.

### WORDS TO KNOW!

**national anthem:** a song played as a mark of loyalty to the nation.

Lots of kids create micronations so they can be in charge for a change. Kevin Baugh founded the Republic of Molossia in 1977, when he was 15 years old. It started as a fun game with a friend. Twenty years later, Baugh bought some property in Nevada and gave Molossia a real-world home. Today, it boasts a national park, a war memorial, a navy (a small blow-up raft), and a space program (a model-rocket launching pad).

Eric Lis of Montreal, Canada was only 5 years old when he created the Aerican Empire. The country is based on silliness, and its flag displays the national symbol, a smiley face. Today, Aerica has hundreds of active citizens, both here on the earth and on several other planets. Lis grew up and became a doctor, but he's still in charge of adding new citizens, getting rid of old ones who don't participate anymore, and keeping everyone up on the news of the empire. In 2012, Aerica celebrated its 25th anniversary.

### FASCINATING FACT

For $70,000 a night, you and 150 of your friends can rent the Principality of Liechtenstein, a microstate roughly the size of Washington, DC, to host a really epic party. That includes your own street names and special money to spend. Townspeople dressed in costumes is extra.

# Fly Your Flag

Flags were originally used in battle so that soldiers could find their leaders. Today, they are often used to represent a country. Flags of 193 countries are flown at the United Nations headquarters in New York City.

A flag design can range from something as simple as Japan's red disc on a white background to highly detailed pictures. Some are just divided into areas of solid

**WORDS TO KNOW!**

**province:** a particular part that a country is divided into.

color, such as the flag of France, which consists of blue, white, and red vertical stripes. Some have sayings, such as the "Don't Tread on Me" flag used during the American Revolution, which showed the words below a drawing of a coiled rattlesnake on a bright yellow background.

Flag designs can feature a plant or animal. Mexico's flag shows an eagle holding a snake in its mouth. The eagle stands on a cactus growing out of a rock surrounded by water—a symbol from the mythology of the ancient Aztecs who lived there.

*Many flags show the sun and stars.*

The flag for the Philippines in the South Pacific has a sun with eight rays for its eight **provinces** and three gold stars for its three main islands.

There are also flags with images of buildings, tools, and weapons. The African country of Mozambique has a garden hoe representing its farmers, crossed with a rifle symbolizing its military, over a book that stands for education. The flag of Oman in the Middle East has an ancient symbol of crossed swords. A few flags have even more unusual designs. Albania's flag has a double-headed eagle. Swaziland's has an ox-hide shield and spears.

## FASCINATING FACT

In 2013, a military historian from the Australian National University proposed a new flag for his country. It would keep the stars of the Southern Cross, but replace the **Union Jack**, which is a reminder that Australia once belonged to Great Britain. In its place would be a boomerang, the popular throwing stick that comes from Australia, and a seven-pointed star filled with dots in the style of native artwork.

# Declaration of Independence

**WORDS TO KNOW!**

**Union Jack:** the national flag of Great Britain, showing red and white crossed stripes on a blue background.

The Declaration of Independence written by Thomas Jefferson and other American leaders in 1776 was one of the most important documents in history. It explained to the world why the 13 colonies in North America that belonged to England wanted to break away and form their own country. But the Americans based their declaration on even older documents, such as the Declaration of Arbroath of 1320, which laid out Scotland's independence from England.

Other countries and groups later borrowed the idea behind America's Declaration of Independence. In 1789, the leaders of the French Revolution wrote their own "Declaration of the Rights of Man," explaining why the people of France wanted to overthrow their king and rule themselves. And the Caribbean country of Haiti declared its independence from France in 1804 after the slaves who lived there led a successful **revolt**.

## What Does the Declaration Say?

The opening words of the Declaration of Independence explained to the world why Americans wanted to be free and separate from England.

*When in the Course of human events, it becomes necessary for one people to dissolve the political bands which have connected them with another, and to assume among the powers of the earth, the separate and equal station to which the Laws of Nature and of Nature's God entitle them, a decent respect to the opinions of mankind requires that they should declare the causes which impel them to the separation.*

*We hold these truths to be self-evident, that all men are created equal, that they are endowed by their Creator with certain unalienable Rights, that among these are Life, Liberty and the pursuit of Happiness. That to secure these rights, Governments are instituted among Men, deriving their just powers from the consent of the governed. That whenever any Form of Government becomes destructive of these ends, it is the Right of the People to alter or to abolish it, and to institute new Government, laying its foundation on such principles and organizing its powers in such form, as to them shall seem most likely to effect their Safety and Happiness.*

# MAKE YOUR OWN
# Flag

Most flags are shaped like a rectangle. They can also be square, triangular, or have a V-shaped "swallow-tail" edge on one side. The flag you create for your micronation can be whatever shape you decide. Use the colors and symbols from your worksheet, or even your country's seal, in your design.

**1** Decide on a design. You can make a few sketches first with paper and pencil if you need to. What are the symbols of your country? How should your flag express the spirit of your country?

**2** Use a sheet of felt as a field or background. Cut it into any shape you want.

**3** Use a thin layer of glue to attach other pieces of felt on top of your background. For instance, you can cut out purple stars to attach to a yellow background. Or buy felt that has a sticky side and just stick the pieces onto the background.

**4** If you like, hang your flag on a wall or attach it to a pole so that it flies over your territory.

---

## Names for Common Flag Designs

- **bicolor:** two colors.
- **tricolor:** three colors.
- **quartered:** divided into two upper and two lower areas.
- **saltire:** x-shaped stripes.
- **canton:** separate box in the upper left-hand corner.
- **stripes:** horizontal, vertical, or diagonal strips of color.
- **serration:** a zigzag pattern.

**BUILD IT YOURSELF**

# WRITE YOUR OWN
## Declaration of Independence

As the head of a new country, you can also write your own declaration of independence. The Declaration of Independence, written by Thomas Jefferson, went through nearly 100 **drafts** before everyone agreed to sign it. Working and reworking a document is an important part of what governments do to reach agreement, usually among many people.

## WORDS TO KNOW!

**draft:** an early version of a document that still needs more work.

## SUPPLIES

- paper and pencil
- scissors
- various kinds of decorative paper
- glue stick
- flat-tipped markers or fancy pens
- official seal (from pages 12–13)

**1** Write a draft of your declaration of independence. Your document should explain what your country stands for and why you decided to create it. This is a rough copy where you can try out different ideas and how you want to put them together.

**2** When you've got the wording just the way you want it, copy it neatly onto decorative paper. You can design it to fit in with your country's theme or make a "traditional" document that looks as though it comes from 1776. One trick to make your writing look old-fashioned is to take a flat-tipped marker and hold it so that it makes fat lines when you move it up and down on the paper and thin lines when you move it across.

**3** Sign your document in grand style. Stamp it with your seal. Don't forget to include your official title as leader of this new country. If your country has other officials, they can sign the declaration with their titles as well. If you have a signing ceremony, make sure to take photos or make a drawing recording it for history.

**4** How will you present your declaration to the world? America's Declaration of Independence was sent out all over the country and was read in public so everyone could hear it. Copies were also hung in public squares. You can let other people know about your new country by giving out copies or putting your declaration on the Internet. If you make a video of yourself reading your document, you can share it with supporters anywhere, anytime.

**BUILD IT YOURSELF**

# CHAPTER TWO

## The Lay of the Land—The Physical Geography of Your Country

**YOUR COUNTRY'S PHYSICAL GEOGRAPHY—THE LAND,** water, **climate**, and living things in an area—can shape its people's lives in important ways. Physical geography plays a role in a country's history and character and affects everyone who lives in the area. It can make the difference between being rich or poor, protected or open to danger, comfortable or struggling. It can be a major factor in whether your citizens have enough to eat and whether people and goods can move easily from one place to another. And it can affect how people and countries interact with each other.

## WORDS TO KNOW!

**climate:** the average weather in an area during a long period of time.

*Here are a few of the ways a country's physical geography can affect its development.*

## Living Off the Land

Where did the first countries develop? In places where the land, water, and weather were good for farming. When the last **Ice Age** ended about 10,000 years ago, people learned how to raise animals and grow plants such as wheat, corn, and rice for food. Their farms were along rivers such as the Indus in India, the Yangtze in China, and the Tigris and Euphrates in the Middle East.

### WORDS TO KNOW!

**Ice Age:** a period of time when ice covers a large part of the earth.

**crop:** a plant grown for food and other uses.

**trade:** the buying, selling, or exchange of goods and services between countries.

**Crops** and animals could feed many people. That meant some people had time to develop other skills they could use to **trade** for food. People learned to make tools, create art, develop writing and math, practice religions, and form armies and governments. Farm communities grew into large settlements, which became towns and cities. Over time, they joined with other settlements to become countries.

## By Land and By Sea

The shape of your country's land and water can have a big impact on its history. **Landforms**—such as mountains—can offer protection from invading armies. Switzerland is a small country in the center of Europe that has been able to avoid war for centuries because of its position high in the rocky Alps. Ancient Egypt was surrounded by deserts and mountains that served as a protective barrier.

> ## WORDS TO KNOW!
>
> **landform:** a natural feature of the earth's surface, such as a mountain or river.
>
> **soil:** the top layer of the earth.

Water is another important feature in a country's development. A coastline with natural harbors can be good for trade and transportation. Rivers can be used for transportation by boat—or by foot or sled if they freeze over in winter. Rivers can carry good **soil** from one area to another when they flood, improving the land for growing crops. They can also power factories and generate electricity.

*Since all living things need water to survive, a country needs a good supply of freshwater found in rivers and lakes.*

But water can also be dangerous. Rising ocean levels due to **climate change** can threaten low-lying cities and towns. During Superstorm Sandy in 2012, the Atlantic Ocean flooded tunnels and streets in New York City and washed away homes and an amusement park in New Jersey.

## WORDS TO KNOW!

**climate change:** changes in the earth's climate patterns, including rising temperatures, which is called global warming.

**sea level:** the level of the surface of the sea.

What are some different types of landforms that you might include in your country?

**Hills, mountains, and plateaus** are areas that are raised above the surrounding land. Hills are usually rounded. Mountains are bigger than hills and may be spiky. Plateaus are high areas that are flat on top.

**Valleys and canyons** are areas that are lower than the surrounding land. Valleys are found between hills or mountains. Canyons have steep, rocky sides.

**Plains** are large flat areas of land.

**Creeks, streams, and rivers** are flowing bodies of freshwater. Creeks are smaller, while rivers are bigger.

## FASCINATING FACT

The Maldives is a country in the Indian Ocean made up of more than 1,200 islands. At their highest point they are barely 3 feet (1 meter) above **sea level**. Some experts say that rising ocean levels could completely swallow up the islands by the year 2050. To bring attention to the threat, in 2009 the president of the Maldives held a meeting underwater! Officials wore diving gear and "spoke" using hand signals.

**Ponds, lakes, seas, and oceans** are bodies of water. Ponds and lakes are filled with freshwater, while seas and oceans are salt water.

**Caves** are underground openings.

**Islands, peninsulas, and isthmuses** are landforms surrounded by water. Islands are completely surrounded, while peninsulas are surrounded on three sides. An isthmus is a narrow strip of land connecting two larger pieces of land.

**Inlets, coves, bays, and gulfs** are sections of a larger body of water surrounded by land on three sides. Inlets are the smallest and gulfs are the largest.

## WORDS TO KNOW!

**geology:** the scientific study of the history and physical nature of the earth.

**tectonic plate:** a large section of the earth's crust that moves on top of the hot melted layer below.

**molten:** melted into liquid by heat.

**magma:** hot liquid rock below the surface of the earth.

## Geology

The **geology** of a country describes what its land is made of. It includes the rocks and soil found at the surface and the different layers beneath the surface. The earth's crust is broken up into giant **tectonic plates**. Beneath these plates is a layer of **molten** rock called **magma**. As the plates shift and move, they slide past each other, spread apart from one another, or push into each other. What happens to the visible landscape when tectonic plates move? It changes! The plate carrying India, for example, is very slowly crashing into Asia, pushing the Himalayan Mountains higher every year.

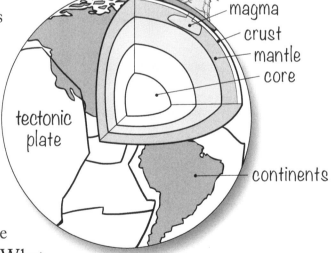

The place where one plate meets another is called a **fault**. Countries that sit atop a fault need to watch out for **earthquakes** and **volcanoes**. Earthquakes are caused by plates slipping past each other. They can cause shaking severe enough to topple buildings and tear bridges apart. They can also trigger enormous waves called tsunamis. An earthquake under the Indian Ocean in 2004 sent tsunamis crashing onto beaches and towns almost 3,000 miles away (5,000 kilometers).

Volcanoes are mountains that form when magma flows up through cracks in the earth's surface. Magma can pour out slowly or it can push out in a powerful **eruption**.

## WORDS TO KNOW!

**fault:** where two tectonic plates meet.

**earthquake:** a sudden movement of the earth's crust caused by tectonic plates slipping along a fault.

**volcano:** a mountain formed by magma or ash forcing its way from deep inside the earth to the surface.

**eruption:** a violent explosion of gas, steam, or ash.

**axis:** the imaginary stick that the earth rotates around.

## Where on Earth Are You?

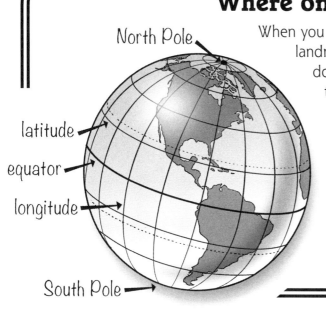

North Pole

latitude

equator

longitude

South Pole

When you want to find where you are on a map, you look for landmarks such as streets, buildings, and rivers. But how do you find where you are on the planet? It helps to understand how the earth is divided up and the words used to describe places on the earth.

**Poles:** Think of the earth as a giant ball with a stick through it. The points where the stick—or **axis**—pokes out at the top and bottom of the ball are the North Pole and South Pole.

**Equator:** The equator is a line drawn around the middle of the earth, halfway between the poles.

When Italy's Mount Vesuvius erupted nearly 2,000 years ago, it buried the city of Pompeii in ash. But volcanoes can also create new land. The Hawaiian Islands in the Pacific Ocean are actually volcanoes rising up from the ocean floor. The soil created from volcanic rock and ash is **fertile** and good for growing crops. What landforms would you choose for your micronation? Are there any landforms you don't want to have? Why?

## Maps

A map is a picture of an area that contains useful information. There are different kinds of maps for different purposes, and many contain more than one type of information. Some maps show roads, cities, borders, landforms, and water. Others use symbols, designs, or colors to indicate population, climate, **elevation**, types of plants or animals, and more.

## WORDS TO KNOW!

**fertile:** describes soil that is good for growing crops.

**elevation:** height above sea level.

**time zone:** a region where all clocks are set to the same time. There are 24 time zones, each one an hour ahead of the zone to the west.

**latitude:** The latitude of a place tells you how far north or south it is from the equator in degrees. The latitude of the equator is zero degrees. The North Pole's latitude is 90 degrees north and the South Pole is 90 degrees south. If you follow one line of latitude around the globe, you will see that it is really a circle. The circles get smaller the closer you get to the poles.

**longitude:** Lines of longitude pass through the North and South poles, dividing the earth like sections of an orange. There are 360 degrees of longitude on the globe—180 east and 180 west. Zero degrees longitude, which passes through the city of Greenwich, England, is called the Prime Meridian. Directly opposite the Prime Meridian on the globe is the International Date Line. The International Date Line marks the place where the day changes. On one side it will be Monday when on the other side of the line it is Sunday. The International Date Line actually zigzags so that no country is divided into two different days! The globe is also divided by longitude into 24 different **time zones**.

You can read a map using the **key**. Maps also have a **compass rose** showing which way is north, so that you can tell how it relates to the earth. **What kinds of maps have you used to learn about different areas?**

**Road Map:** Have you ever used a road map to find your way around when you were on a trip? It shows things such as towns, cities, airports, stores, and restaurants, as well as parks, monuments, and tourist attractions. Major highways are shown as heavy lines and smaller roads as thinner lines. Some maps also show railroad lines as a thin line with little rails and recreation trails for hiking, biking, or skiing as dotted lines.

Relief    Road    Political

**Political Map:** A political map tells you the shape of a country's borders, its size in comparison to other countries, and where it is on the earth. Usually it shows neighboring countries and any states, provinces, or other divisions within the country itself. Sometimes different countries or states are shown in different colors. A capital city is often shown as a star, while other cities are marked by a circle or other symbol in different sizes, depending on the size of the city.

> ## WORDS TO KNOW!
>
> **key:** a chart that explains all the symbols used on a map.
>
> **compass rose:** a circle drawn on a map to show north, south, east, and west.

**Physical Maps and Relief Maps:** A physical map looks something like a painting of the countryside as seen from overhead. Rivers, lakes, and oceans are blue. Low-lying areas covered with vegetation are green. Higher areas and dry deserts are shown as yellow or brown. And the tops of very high mountains are shown as white, as if they were covered in snow. A relief map is **three-dimensional (3-D)**, usually made out of a stiff plastic or other material, and has bumps of various heights to indicate hills and mountains.

# WORDS TO KNOW!

**three-dimensional (3-D):** an image that has length, width, and height, and is raised off the flat page.

**cartography:** the art and science of making maps.

**surveying tools:** special instruments for taking measurements over long distances.

**remote sensing:** measuring the features of the earth over long distances with cameras and other tools.

**GPS:** Global Positioning System, a system of satellites, computers, and receivers that can determine the exact location of a receiver anywhere on the planet.

**data:** information in the form of facts and numbers.

**GIS:** Geographic Information System, a type of computer program used for making maps that can show different kinds of information.

# Mapmaking: Yesterday and Today

The science of mapmaking is called **cartography**. Ancient maps were not very exact because measurements were not very exact. **Surveying tools** helped make maps more accurate. Today, mapmakers use **remote sensing** such as **GPS** and photographs taken by satellites high above the earth as the basis for maps. They can combine these images with all kinds of **data** about a place—for example, what plants grow there, how much houses cost, or the age of the people living in an area. This is all put together by computer using **GIS**. Printed maps do still exist. But many people now use maps on computers and other devices, which let you zoom in and out and select the kind of information you want to see. Can you think of situations when computerized maps are more useful? How about paper maps?

## FASCINATING FACT

Scientists believe that millions of years ago all the land on the earth was joined into one large continent, which they call Pangaea. As the earth's tectonic plates shifted and moved over time, Pangaea split apart into the pieces that form the continents. That's why South America looks as if it would fit into Africa like a puzzle piece.

Africa

South America

## Climate

Different regions on the planet have different weather patterns, or climates. Climate includes things such as the normal range of temperature, rainfall and snowfall, and wind.

### WORDS TO KNOW!

**Arctic Circle:** a line of latitude near the North Pole.

*How do you think climate determines what kind of clothing people wear, what their houses are like, and what types of food they eat?*

People in cold climates near the North and South poles need to bundle up in heavy layers. They need homes that will hold in the heat. And the growing season for crops is short. People living near or within the **Arctic Circle** may not be able to farm at all, but instead rely on hunting, fishing, and eating wild plants.

In hotter climates near the equator, people can wear lighter clothing all year long, but they need to protect themselves from the sun. To stay cool, they need buildings that let in the breeze. In a rainy climate, people might build houses on stilts to prevent water from getting inside. Growing crops may be difficult in an area that is hot and dry as in a desert.

The climate of a place depends on where it is on the planet. The earth is hotter at the equator and colder at the poles. That's because of the way the earth travels around the sun. The equator gets hit directly with the sun's rays—which send out heat, light, and energy. But the sun's rays hit the poles at an angle. The earth's axis also has a slight tilt, which gives the areas between the poles and the equator their seasons. When a pole is tilted toward the sun, that part of the earth has summer. When it's tilted away, there's winter.

The **rotation** of the earth causes air and water **currents**. Currents can bring heat or cold from one region to another. Wind currents can pick up water droplets from the ocean and let them fall over the land, creating rain and snow. And they can pick up dust and debris from one area and drop them on another, affecting the air quality for plants and animals and blocking some of the sun's light and heat from reaching the earth. Water currents, such as the Gulf Stream, can bring warm water north from the equator. Currents can also move cold water to warmer areas.

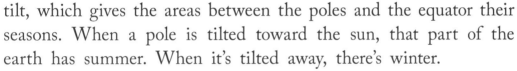

## WORDS TO KNOW!

**rotation:** a turn all the way around.

**current:** the steady flow of water or air in one direction.

Landforms can have a large effect on climate. Mountains can create "rain shadows" by blocking wind currents that blow in from the ocean, so one side has a moist climate, while the other side is dry. Areas in the center of a large continent tend to be dry because winds can't carry water that far from the coastlines.

## WORDS TO KNOW!

**atmosphere:** the blanket of air surrounding the earth.

**species:** a group of plants or animals that are closely related and look the same.

The climate at the top of a mountain is often quite different from the bottom because of the difference in elevation. The higher a place is above sea level, the thinner its **atmosphere**. The atmosphere is what holds in the sun's heat and keeps the earth warm. The less atmosphere, the less heat.

## FASCINATING FACT

In September 2013, a massive earthquake in Pakistan left behind a new island offshore. Such "mud volcano" islands usually last only a few weeks before they wash away.

## Unclaimed Territory

If you want to start a land-based micronation, where can you put it? Almost every place on Earth already belongs to someone. But there are still some options.

**Snag a new volcanic island:** The volcanic islands in Hawaii took thousands of years to form. But volcanic islands can pop up almost overnight. Surtsey is a volcanic island off the coast of Iceland that appeared in 1963 and kept growing for four years. Today, it is home to hundreds of **species** of wildlife.

**Find some abandoned land:** Easter Island in the Pacific Ocean is 1,100 miles (1,770 kilometers) from its nearest neighbor. It is famous for the giant, carved stone heads called *moai*, created by the Polynesia settlers who lived there for many centuries. But as the population grew, the people used up all the palm trees that once covered the island. Eventually, almost everyone moved away, leaving about 400 carvings behind. In the 1700s, the island was claimed by Chile, and today about 2,000 people live there. There is still plenty of space!

**Make your own:** English artist Reishee Sowa wanted his own tropical island, so he built one off the coast of Mexico out of empty plastic soda bottles. He filled nets with about 100,000 empty discarded plastic bottles to support the plywood and bamboo base of his

island, which has three beaches, a house, two ponds, a solar-powered waterfall and river, and a wave-powered washing machine. Tours of Joyxee Island are available to the public.

**Stake your claim on some unwanted territory:** *Terra nullius* is a Latin phrase meaning "no one owns it." It was the excuse some countries used to declare themselves in charge of land they found in places such as Australia—even if the native people already living there disagreed. There are a few pieces of *terra nullius* around. The largest is a slice of the continent of Antarctica called Marie Byrd Land. The territory is so remote, no real country wants it. Other bits of *terra nullius* include Bir Tawil, a tiny piece of desert between Egypt and Sudan. Each country claims it belongs to the other.

# MAKE YOUR OWN
## Microcache Treasure Hunt

When you're hunting for treasure, it helps to know how to read a map, measure distances, look for landmarks and signs, and find directions with a compass. In this game, you will hide a treasure related to your micronation in a cache or hidden storage place. See if players can follow your written directions to find it.

**1** Make your microcache by putting your micronation's token inside some kind of container. If you are going to hide it outside, make sure the container is waterproof and sturdy.

**2** Where will you hide your microcache? Be sure to get permission before putting it on private property. If you are hiding it in a public place, such as a park, look for a spot where it won't be noticed by anyone passing by. Under the roots of a tree or in the middle of a pile of rocks is a good hiding place. In a city, you may be able to hide it in a crack of a wall or behind a bush.

**3** Pick a starting point for your microcache hunt. Then pick two or more points along the way as checkpoints. Players have to find their way from one checkpoint to the next until they reach the microcache at the end. You may decide to make the path of your treasure hunt twist and turn a little, rather than have it lead directly to the prize. For checkpoints, look for a sign, a tree, a large rock, or anything that will stay in one place and be easy to pick out.

**4** Begin to write out your instructions by walking through it yourself, taking notes as you go. To help players get from one checkpoint to the next, you

## WORDS TO KNOW!

**coordinates:** a set of numbers or directions that tell you where a place is.

need to give them two **coordinates**—the direction and the distance. If the microcache hunter needs to look down or up to find the landmark, you will need to include a third coordinate to tell them that, too.

**5** To find out which direction players must walk, use a compass. The magnetic arrow always points toward the North Pole, because the earth is a giant magnet that aligns other magnets to its own magnetic field. Hold your compass so that the line marked N for north is pointing in the same direction as the north end of the arrow. Holding the compass steady, turn your head to look toward the place where players will be heading next. Find the line on the compass that points toward that place to get the direction.

**6** You can measure the distance to the next checkpoint in steps. Put one foot directly in front of the other so the heel touches the toe of the foot behind it to count the number of steps to the next point. To be more exact, convert the number of steps into feet or meters by measuring the length of your foot (in inches or centimeters) and multiplying that number by the number of steps. Divide the result by 12 to get the distance in feet or by 100 for meters.

**7** If your directions are correct, anyone should be able to use them to find your microcache. Ask them to give you proof that they found it by answering a question about the prize, such as, "Whose face is on the coin?" or by sending you a photo of it.

## FASCINATING FACT

This microcache game is a combination of two popular treasure hunt games called letterboxing and geocaching. You can find out more about these activities by going to www.letterboxing.org and www.geocaching.com.

**BUILD IT YOURSELF**

# MAKE YOUR OWN
# Multilayered Map of Your Micronation

There is a lot to think about as you decide what your micronation's physical geography will be like. Does your micronation have bodies of water, mountains, jungles, or deserts? Does it contain fertile farmland or valuable **natural resources**? What is its climate like? Are there animals that can be used for food, clothing, or work? What plants grow there?

What kinds of crops do people raise? Is there wood for building or for fuel? Is it prone to scorching hot spells or driving rainstorms?

Draw a multilayered map so you can look at just the things you need. Each layer shows just one kind of information. When you put one layer over another, you can see several different kinds of information at once. Your map uses paper, but it is based on the same idea as GIS computer maps.

**SUPPLIES**

- pens, permanent markers, or pencils, both black and colored
- stiff paper or cardboard
- 4 sheets of tracing paper or acetate, or clear plastic loose leaf sheet protectors split into two sheets
- tape

1 Your map will include basic physical information, plus up to four other kinds of information. The bottom layer shows the shape of your micronation. Use the stiff paper as your base. Draw the border around your micronation. Make the lines nice and dark, so they show through the upper layers.

2 Add the first layer to your map by taking one sheet of tracing paper or plastic and cutting it a bit smaller than the base map. Place it next to the base map on your work table so one edge matches up with the map. Attach a strip of tape over the seam where the tracing paper meets the map. Then fold the tracing paper along the seam to create a flap that can be flopped over the map and off again. Add up to three more layers the same way. Tape each one along a different edge of the base map. That way, you can lift them all up, or just put down the ones you want to see.

**3** Use the first layer of your map to show the physical features of your micronation. Use color and symbols and include lakes, rivers, mountains, deserts, forests—any physical feature of the planet's surface that is found within the borders of your tiny country. Make sure the colors are strong enough to show through the layers of tracing paper.

**4** Decide what other kinds of information would be useful to someone looking at a map of your country as you create the layers. The first step is to trace over the border of the country onto the new layer, so you can match them up again. If you are using pencil on tracing paper, be careful not to tear it. For a political map, mark the major cities, towns, and state borders.

To make a road map, draw highways, railroads, or any other route you want connecting cities and other popular locations, such as a beach or national monument. You can also make a map that shows where people speak different languages or symbols to show what kinds of foods they like to eat. Your map can show any kind of the information that can be indicated using different colors, patterns (such as stripes or dots), and symbols.

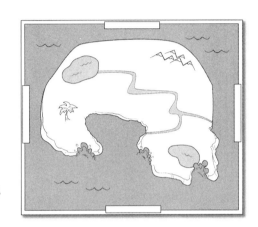

# FASCINATING FACT

Because the earth is round like a ball, it's hard to show the whole world on a flat map. If you draw it so that the lines of longitude are straight up and down—instead of getting closer toward the poles, as they do in real life—any land near the poles will look stretched out. A map projection tries to solve this problem by "peeling the skin" of the earth like an orange and flattening it out. This keeps the continents closer to their actual shape and size. But the most accurate world map is a globe, because it is three-dimensional like the earth.

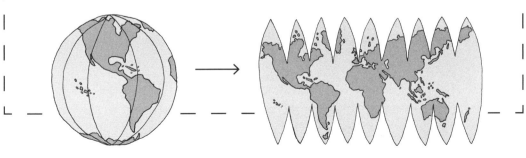

# CHAPTER THREE

## Law and Order—How Your Country Runs

### WHO IS IN CHARGE OF YOUR MICRONATION?

Who makes up the rules? The type of government
you choose will establish the relationship between
your country's leaders and its citizens.

In its most simple form, a government is a system that helps a group of people live and work together. The earliest forms of government were **clans** and **tribes**. People related by marriage and other ties banded together for protection and to hunt or raise food together. They were led by the oldest, strongest, wisest members. These groups grew in size by becoming **allies** with neighboring groups or by conquering them and taking them over. As they became more powerful, they developed systems to help keep order, organized armies and workers, and created rules that told people how to act. These became the first governments.

## WORDS TO KNOW!

**clan:** a large group of related families.

**tribe:** a group of clans with the same language, customs, and beliefs.

**ally:** a country that agrees to help and support another country.

**executive:** the branch of government that includes the leader and the advisors who run the country.

**legislative:** the branch of government that makes the laws.

**judicial:** the branch of government consisting of courts with judges who decide if laws have been broken.

# Government Today

The job of a government is usually broken up into three parts. The **executive** branch includes the leader and the advisors who run the government. The **legislative** branch makes the laws. In the **judicial** branch, judges decide if laws have been broken.

The three separate branches of government in the United States each has some control over the other two. This system of checks and balances keeps any one of the branches from becoming too powerful.

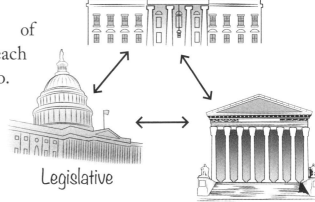

Executive

Legislative

Judicial

In other countries, a king may run the government, make the laws, and decide if laws have been broken. Or the head of the legislative branch may run the government, while a king represents the executive branch but doesn't really have any power.

Governments can be described by the kind of leader who runs the country, the way leaders are chosen, or how much ordinary citizens are involved with how things run. **Which of these types of government would you choose for your micronation?**

**Monarchy:** Monarchs are rulers such as kings, queens, and emperors who hold their positions for life. Usually, the position is hereditary, which means it is passed down from parent to child or other member of the royal family. In an absolute monarchy, the ruler has unlimited control of the country. The first empires to develop in the Middle East, India, and China were run this way.

Today, it is more common to have a constitutional monarchy. In these countries, the king or queen serves as the **symbolic** head, but **elected** officials actually run the government. Countries such as the Netherlands, Japan, and Norway, are constitutional monarchies.

**WORDS TO KNOW!**

**symbolic:** something that is important because of what it stands for or represents.

**elect:** to choose someone by vote.

However, there are still absolute monarchies around, including the Sultanate of Brunei in the Middle East, Bhutan in the Himalayas, and the Kingdom of Tonga in the Pacific.

**Theocracy:** In a theocracy, the head of the government is also the head of the country's official religion. Some theocratic leaders claim to govern by divine right, meaning their power to rule comes from heaven. The pharaohs of ancient Egypt claimed to be gods themselves.

Only a few theocracies exist today. Vatican City, located within the city of Rome, Italy, is ruled by the pope, who is also the head of the Roman Catholic church. This tiny piece of land is all that remains of the once-vast empire controlled by the church. In the Islamic country of Iran, an ayatollah is the religious authority who holds the title of Supreme Leader of the country. But there is also an elected president who holds some of the power in the government.

## FASCINATING FACT

In 2013, Pope Benedict XVI became the first pope in 600 years to give up his job before his death. As usual, church officials met in secret in Vatican City to elect a new pope. In keeping with tradition, they sent a puff of white smoke up through the chimney of the Sistine Chapel to signal that a new leader, Pope Francis, had been chosen. People around the world watched for the smoke signal live, on the Internet.

## Government in Exile

The Dalai Lama, the head of the Buddhist religion for Tibetan people, was also the ruler of Tibet until the country was invaded by China in 1959. The Dalai Lama fled to India, where he set up a **government in exile**. Since then, he has spoken out in favor of world peace and worked to convince the Chinese to allow the Tibetan people to rule themselves.

## WORDS TO KNOW!

**government in exile:** a government that tries to keep running after it has been forced out of the country.

**Totalitarian:** A totalitarian government is controlled by one **political party**. Membership in the party is limited, and members get special privileges. Ordinary citizens have no rights or freedoms and must follow the state's orders. The party may be run by a **dictator** or a small group of people who rule like a dictator. Citizens in totalitarian countries are not allowed to protest against the government or have any say in how things are run.

If **elections** are held, people are forced to vote for the ruling party. The government may control the supply of food, clothing, household supplies, and cars or other means of transportation. Travel inside or outside the country may be limited. News, books, movies, and access to the Internet may be **censored**. Totalitarian countries today include Cuba and North Korea.

**Democracy:** In the last 50 years, most of the countries of the world have broken free of other forms of government and become democracies. In a **democracy**, citizens select their leaders by voting in elections with a choice of **candidates**. The first known democratic government was formed in 594 **BCE** in ancient Greece, where a leader named Solon wrote laws to help different clans work together peacefully.

## WORDS TO KNOW!

**political party:** a group that holds particular ideas about how to run the government.

**dictator:** a ruler with unlimited control whose power comes from the military.

**election:** a vote where citizens get to choose a leader.

**censor:** when the government blocks citizens from seeing certain information.

**democracy:** a government where citizens pick the leaders and have a say in how things are run.

**candidate:** a person who runs for an office in the government.

**BCE:** put after a date, BCE stands for Before Common Era and counts down to zero. CE stands for Common Era and counts up from zero. These non-religious terms correspond to BC and AD.

Direct

In a direct democracy, voters make all the decisions themselves. This type of democracy only works in places with small populations. In Switzerland, where the population of the entire country is smaller than that of New York City, citizens have the right to vote directly to approve national laws.

LAWS

presentational

In a representational democracy, citizens elect someone to represent them and make decisions on their behalf. In the United States, the two houses of Congress— the **Senate** and the **House of Representatives**—have the power to create laws, decide how to spend money, and declare war. American voters also choose a president to sign laws, lead the military, and represent the country worldwide. In other representational democracies, such as Germany and Canada, voters elect a representative to a governing group called a parliament. Members of parliament then choose a prime minister as head of government.

LAWS

## WORDS TO KNOW!

**Senate:** the legislative body in the United States that has two representatives for every state.

**House of Representatives:** the legislative body in the United States that has representatives from 435 districts across the country. Each district has roughly the same population. Some states have more districts than others.

**invasion:** when one country or group moves in to take over another country.

## FASCINATING FACT

What do you call it when a country has no government at all? Anarchy! A country can fall into a state of anarchy because of revolution, civil war, **invasion**, or other fighting. Some people, called libertarians, think people should take care of themselves with no help from the government.

# Political Parties

Political parties play an important role in government. True democracies have more than one political party. Each party has a platform, which is a set of beliefs or goals that candidates promise to uphold if elected. When parties with opposing ideas work together, they often come up with a good **compromise** that fits with the beliefs and goals of the **majority** of the country. But when their ideas are so different that no compromise can be reached, the government can grind to a halt. In the United States, it's possible to have the president belong to one party, while one or both houses of Congress is controlled by the other party. Countries that use the parliamentary system sometimes have more than two parties, but the prime minister is always a member of the majority party (or from a group of **minority** parties working together).

## WORDS TO KNOW!

**compromise:** an agreement reached by two sides working together.

**majority:** most of the people or voters.

**minority:** the side with fewer supporters.

**amend:** to change a law.

**repeal:** to cancel a law.

**enforce:** to carry out a law.

# Constitutions

Most countries of the world have a constitution to describe how the government is set up. But the real purpose of a constitution is to clarify what the government is and is not allowed to do. A constitution is a set of laws that the government must follow, and it includes instructions for how those laws are made, **amended**, **repealed**, and **enforced**.

*The constitution usually includes the most important ideas about running the government. But there are also things that are considered to be part of the constitution even though they are not written down.*

The Constitution of the United States lists the rights and duties that belong to the **federal** government. Everything not listed belongs to the states or directly to the people. Because that leaves a lot of room for disagreement, the **Supreme Court** often has to decide what the Constitution means.

It is not written directly into the Constitution, but the Supreme Court has ruled that citizens have a right to privacy. This means the government cannot go into homes and tell people how to live. Are there parts of the U.S. constitution that you might like to include in a constitution for your own micronation? How will they be different?

## WORDS TO KNOW!

**federal:** national, covering the whole country.

**Supreme Court:** the highest court of law in a country, with the top panel of judges.

## Bill of Rights

Not every country has a bill of rights. America's Bill of Rights was added in the form of 10 amendments after the Constitution was written. But newer constitutions often include a very detailed bill of rights. Experts disagree about whether it is helpful or dangerous to include a large number of specific rights. South Africa's Bill of Rights includes the right to higher education such as college, as well as the right to be free from slavery. Critics say such long lists make all rights included seem equally important and any that are not included seem less important.

## Preamble From the U.S. Constitution

A preamble is an introduction to a document that states the reasons for creating it. The preamble to the U.S. Constitution sets the tone for the rest of the document.

*We the People, of the United States, in Order to form a more perfect Union, establish Justice, insure domestic Tranquility, provide for the common defense, promote the general Welfare, and secure the Blessings of Liberty to ourselves and our Posterity, do ordain and establish this Constitution for the United States of America.*

**Three countries in the world have no written constitution.**

**Great Britain:** In Great Britain, there are documents such as the Magna Carta, written in 1215, which limit the power of the monarch, as well as a tradition of people's rights going back even earlier.

**New Zealand:** In New Zealand, the Treaty of Waitangi between Britain and the native Māori people is one of several chief documents that serve as a constitution.

**Israel:** This country was formed in 1945 as a home for Jewish people after World War II. Disagreements over the role of religious law in the country is one reason no constitution has been written.

## FASCINATING FACT

The U.S. Constitution, the first national constitution in the world, was written in 1787. Today, it includes 27 amendments, including one that made slavery illegal and another that lowered the voting age from 21 to 18.

# WRITE YOUR OWN
## Code of Laws

The constitution lays out laws the government must follow. But countries also need a code of laws for its citizens. Why are good laws important? How strict do you think laws should be? In 2013, the mayor of New York City tried to ban super-sized sodas. What do you think he was trying to accomplish?

Laws are not always serious. In Arizona, a law says that donkeys cannot sleep in bathtubs. In California, nobody is allowed to ride a bicycle in a swimming pool. The Aerican Empire micronation has its own set of laws. One of them is Murphy's Law, which follows.

*In light of the future being for the most part unknown;*

*In light of the fact that no person or persons can predict the needs that a government will have to fill;*

*In light of the fact that whatever can go wrong, will go wrong;*

*The Aerican Senate does hereby put forth this law.*

*That as the need arises, due to changing structure, science, economy, or circumstance, that the Senate will assume power as is needed that it may best fulfill the needs of its people.*

*This document is set forth as law, by the Emperor of the Aerican Empire, by the Senate of the Aerican Empire, in accordance with all laws and statutes put forth by said Empire.*

**1** What are some laws that you think are important for your micronation? What will help people stay safe and get along and live a happy life? Be sure to state clearly what the law allows the citizens to do or what it prohibits them from doing. Don't forget to describe the punishment for breaking the law.

**2** Hold a signing ceremony for your new laws. Use your official seal to stamp the law when it is signed!

**BUILD IT YOURSELF**

# DRAFT YOUR OWN
## Constitution

Your micronation's constitution is a plan for how your government will work. It should include a preamble to explain what your country is about and directions for setting everything up. You can also decide whether or not to include a written bill of rights to protect your people's rights. Look up the constitutions of the United States and other real countries or micronations to get an idea of what you might want to include.

**1** Write a short preamble that describes your country's theme, goals, and values. If your constitution will have a bill of rights that spells out what freedoms your country's citizens enjoy, write that up as a list or in paragraphs.

## FASCINATING FACT

The original hand-written Constitution of the United States is only four pages long. They used very small writing.

**2** In the next part, describe your system of government. You can make an organizational chart to help plan how it will work. On a piece of paper, make three columns: Legislative, Executive, and Judicial.

**3** At the top of each column, draw a box tall enough for three or four lines of writing. Inside, write the title of the person or persons in charge of that branch. The same person can be in charge of two or three. If there are advisors who help the top person, write the title of the advisor under the person in charge and draw a line connecting them.

| Legislative | Executive | Judicial |
|---|---|---|
| **Senate & House** | **President** | **Supreme Court** |
| | Vice President — Cabinet | \| Federal Courts |
| Make laws | | Hold trials to decide if laws have been broken |
| Represent the citizens in the government | Represent your country to the world and make treaties with other countries | |
| Decide how money will be spent | Command the military or protect the country with other methods | |

## Preamble From the Northern Forest Archipelago Constitution

The Constitution of the Northern Forest Archipelago micronation reflects the importance of nature to its ruler, King James III.

*We, the creatures and plants and rocks and rivers of the wilderness, in order to pursue the goals spelled out in this constitution; do establish the Northern Forest Archipelago on this, the twenty-first day of September, in the year 1998. Let it be known both far and near that the Northern Forest Archipelago, an independent and sovereign state, will be a state guided by respect for all.*

**4** In each column of your chart, under the boxes stating who is in charge, list the things you want that branch of your government to do. These are duties and responsibilities. They can include: represent your country to the world and make treaties with other countries, represent the citizens in the government, command the military or protect the country with other methods, make laws, hold trials to decide if laws have been broken, and decide how money will be spent.

**5** When your chart is done, write up your plan for government in your constitution in paragraph form. You can follow the U.S. Constitution and break them down into articles and sections or make up your own system.

**6** The rest of your constitution can include information on other things your country needs.

* **Citizenship:** How do people become citizens?
* **Leadership:** Who can be leader in your country?
* **Voting:** Are there elections in your country? When are they held and who gets to vote in them?
* **Systems:** Does the government provide education, transportation, or health care to citizens in your country? (See Chapter 5 for more ideas.)
* **Amendments:** What is the process for changing and updating the constitution?

# MAKE YOUR OWN
# Passport

A passport is a document the government issues to you as proof that you are a citizen. It is mostly used when you cross the border from one country to another. Many micronations sell passports as souvenirs. The Conch Republic in Florida claims that people have traveled all over the world using their passports. Passports generally look like little books with your name, address, date of birth, and other information. There is a photo to show that the passport belongs to you. The passport also contains several blank pages. When you cross a border, the border official will stamp your passport with the country's seal. A passport is a nice reminder of your travels outside your own country!

1 Use the heavy paper to make the cover. A passport should be small enough to fit in your pocket. Cut out a rectangle about 8 inches by 5 inches (20 centimeters by 12 centimeters). Fold it in half to make a cover around 4 inches by 5 inches (10 centimeters by 12 centimeters).

2 Use the lightweight paper for the inside pages. Cut out two or three sheets the same way as the cover. If you want, trim the inside pages so they are a little bit smaller. Put the inside pages in a pile, and fold them all at the same time.

3 Open up the folded inside pages and cover. Place the pile of inside pages into the cover so that the folds match up. Use the stapler to staple them all together along the fold so that none of the pages fall out.

BUILD IT YOURSELF

# Citizenship

There are different ways to become a citizen of a country. Any person born in the United States is a citizen. You can also become a citizen if one of your parents is a citizen or if you marry a citizen. In order to be **naturalized**, you have to pass a test on U.S. government and history and you must be at least 18 years old, a resident living in the United States for at least five years, English speaking, and someone of good moral character who has not committed any crimes. At the naturalization ceremony, you must stand before a judge and swear an oath of allegiance, saying that you will support and be loyal to the United States and give up any foreign title.

**4** Close the passport and hold it with the fold to your left. Write "Passport" and the name of your country on the cover. Leave space for your micronation's official seal.

**5** Turn the passport so that the fold is at the top. Open it up, and glue the photo along the left edge of the first inside page. Then write your name and other information next to it.

**6** You can add border-crossing stamps on the other pages if you like. Do a search for the different stamps used by real countries for inspiration. Stamps are usually done in different shapes, sizes, and colors. Overlap them on the page to make an interesting design.

## FASCINATING FACT

Some societies use symbols that show everyone is equal. In the northwestern United States, Native American people pass around a talking stick during meetings so everyone has a turn to be heard.

**BUILD IT YOURSELF**

# MAKE YOUR OWN
## Sash as a Symbol of Authority

Leaders have used various symbols to show that they were in charge. When Elizabeth II became queen of Great Britain in a **coronation** ceremony in 1953, she was given symbols of authority, including a **scepter** with a cross to represent Christianity, a rod topped with the figure of a dove to represent peace, and a coronation ring. A solid gold crown was placed on her head. Symbols of authority in different parts of the world include a chain necklace, a sash, a robe, or an animal skin.

### WORDS TO KNOW!

**coronation:** a ceremony to crown a monarch.

**scepter:** a ceremonial stick carried by a monarch as a sign of authority.

**mace:** a ceremonial stick carried by an official as a sign of authority in a legislature.

Here are directions for making a sash, a fabric strip worn across the chest. It is a symbol of authority often used by both monarchs and elected officials.

**1** Choose some fabric for your sash that represents your micronation. It can be in your national colors or with a print that relates to your theme. The leader of a jungle micronation might choose fabric covered in a green leafy pattern, for instance. You can buy a length of fabric in a sewing shop, reuse old scarves, cut up recycled cloth sheets, or put together strips of ribbon.

**2** To figure out how much fabric you will need for your sash, put the end of the tape measure on one shoulder. Then pull the tape measure across your chest to your opposite hip. Take that measurement, double it, and add about 1 foot (25 centimeters). That is about how long your sash needs to be.

measure this distance

**measure this distance**

③ To get the width, measure the distance from the tip of your shoulder to your neck. Write down the two measurements.

④ Take your fabric and cut a piece the length and width of your measurements. Make it a little bigger all around if you want to finish the edges by folding them down and stitching or gluing them closed. If your piece of fabric isn't long enough for your sash, cut several shorter strips in the right width. Connect them with fabric glue or stitch them together with needle and thread.

⑤ You might want to find someone to help you with this next step! Take your strip of fabric and hang it over your right shoulder and so the ends are even. Now take the half in front and cross it over your chest at an angle, so it touches your left hip. Make it just loose enough to be comfortable. There should be a little bit of fabric left over. Next, reach behind you for the other end of the sash and cross it over your back to your left hip. Cross the two ends to form a large X. Fasten them with a safety pin. You'll probably want to cover or replace the safety pin in front with something more official looking, like a fancy pin or button, large badge, or giftwrap bow.

⑥ If you like, add more decorations along the sash by sewing or gluing on play jewelry, small toys, old medals, or anything else that shows you are the leader of your country.

## FASCINATING FACT

In the Canadian province of Alberta, the first **mace** used by the legislature in 1906 was made of an iron, a plumbing pipe, pieces of a brass bed, the plumbing float from a flush toilet, and mermaid-shaped handles from a shaving mug! The shaving mug mace was used for 50 years.

# CHAPTER FOUR

# The Material World—Your Country's Economy

## WHERE DOES YOUR COUNTRY GET ITS WEALTH?

And who decides how to spend it? The answer depends on the type of economy your country has. By definition, a country must have an organized economy so that people, companies, and the government can exchange goods and services. The economic system a country chooses plays a big role in how its people live and get along with the government and each other.

# What Is an Economy and How Does It Work?

Whenever something of value is transferred from one owner to another, you have an economy. Something of value can be a good, which is an item that someone wants, such as candy you buy at a store. Or it can be a service, which is something one person does for another, such as when your neighbors pay you to walk their dog. An economy is the way people get the things they need and want, such as a home, a new pair of shoes, or their car repaired.

The economic system of a country describes the way it makes goods and the services available to its people. **There are two common systems.**

## WORDS TO KNOW!

**free market economy:** a system where people are free to buy and sell things they own.

**profit:** the amount gained by transferring something of value to someone else for more than it cost.

**Free Market Economy:** A **free market economy** is based on the idea of private property belonging to one person, family, or group. People can exchange goods and services with each other by buying, selling, and trading. Private businesses try to make a **profit**.

*The more a person or company owns, the richer and more powerful they become.*

$1.00 per lb.

$1.50 per lb.

Prices in a free market economy can go up and down depending on **supply and demand**. If a lot of **consumers** want a product but it is in short supply, prices may go up. If demand goes down, prices can drop too. **Competition** from more than one supplier can help keep prices from getting too high. But a **monopoly** can set any price it likes. Companies can also create more demand by using advertising and marketing to make products looks more appealing.

In a free market economy, people can work for themselves and get the benefit of what they produce or they may work for an **employer**, who keeps the profits. In exchange, employers pay their workers. The amount paid also follows the law of supply and demand. When there are a lot of people looking for work and not enough jobs for all of them, pay can go down. Workers who join together in a **union** can have more power to ask employers for higher pay than workers might get on their own.

## WORDS TO KNOW!

**supply and demand:** the rule that prices go up and down depending on how much there is of something and how much people want it.

**consumer:** a person who buys goods and services.

**competition:** trying to get something another person or company wants at the same time.

**monopoly:** when there is only one supplier or group of suppliers for a good or service.

**employer:** a person or company that hires people to work for pay.

**union:** a group that represents workers when dealing with the employer.

**Command Economy:** In a **command economy**, everything belongs to the government, which can be a political party, a dictator, or an absolute monarch and members of the ruling class. The government decides what goods will be made and what services will be provided. Decisions may be based on making good use of natural resources and creating jobs for workers. Meeting the needs and wants of consumers may be less important. Everyone works for the government, which decides how much workers will be paid. The government also keeps any profits. People get all of the things they need from the government or companies owned by the government. That includes food, clothing, housing, schooling, news and information, and health care.

*In reality, most countries use some combination of these two systems.*

> # WORDS TO KNOW!
>
> **command economy:** a system in which everything belongs to the government, which decides what is made and how much it costs.
>
> **capitalist:** a free market system.
>
> **communist:** a system in which everything is owned and run by the government.
>
> **socialist:** combining capitalist and communist methods. The government provides services but private property is allowed.

**Capitalist** countries mostly use a free market economy. **Communist** countries, as well as absolute monarchies and dictatorships, mostly use a command economy. **Socialist** countries use both. They allow people to run their own businesses, but the government also provides many of the services people use, such as transportation and health care. However, capitalist countries also use a command economic model when they control the use of natural resources or require people to serve in the military. And communist countries follow capitalist rules of supply and demand when they do business with other countries.

What type of economy would you choose for your micronation? Would you choose an economy that's different from the United States economy?

## Can a Country Have a Traditional Economy?

In a **traditional economy**, only personal possessions such as clothing are considered private property. The community provides things such as food and shelter to all. The Iroquois, a Native American tribe in the northeastern United States, once lived this way. Up to 20 families shared a single longhouse. But because no one owns the land, a traditional economy does not fit the definition of a country. A real country requires ownership of land, so a country can't have a traditional economy.

## WORDS TO KNOW!

**traditional economy:** a system where a group of people all work together and almost everything belongs to the group.

**nonrenewable:** not able to be replaced.

**raw material:** something used to make something else. Natural resources are raw materials.

**minerals:** naturally occurring solids found in rocks and in the ground. Rocks are made of minerals. Gold and diamonds are precious minerals.

## Natural Resources

A country gets part of its wealth from its natural resources. The harder the natural resource is to find or collect, or the more demand there is for it, the more the resource is worth. Some natural resources are **nonrenewable**. We can't make more of them and that means when they are used up they're gone. Countries that have good supplies of valuable **raw materials** can use them to make goods or trade them.

Some of the most important natural resources include freshwater for drinking and growing crops, the **mineral** phosphorus used to make fertilizer, and rare earth magnets used in computers and cell phones. Others include salt for preparing food, precious metals such as gold and silver and gems such as diamonds and rubies for jewelry and other uses, and minerals such as iron and titanium for building materials and tools. Coal, oil, and natural gas are used for heat, light, electricity, to run machines and vehicles, and to make plastics.

## FASCINATING FACT

Until 1890, the main natural resource of the U.S. territory of Howland Island in the Pacific was guano, also known as bird poop! Guano is used by farmers as fertilizer, but the methods used to get the guano killed or scared away the birds that produced it. That turned guano into a nonrenewable resource.

# Where Does a Country Get Its Money?

If you want some money to go to the movies, you might offer to mow the lawn for a family in your neighborhood. When a country needs money to run things and provide services for its people, it can't go out and get a job. A country needs to raise **revenue**. Where does the money come from?

**Fees:** Governments charge people a **fee** for **licenses** and some services.

**Taxes:** Governments charge many kinds of **taxes**. Income tax is based on how much money you make. Property tax is based on the value of your land and buildings. Sales tax is based on how much you pay for a good or service. Businesses also pay taxes on their profits.

**Trade:** For countries, trade means **imports** and **exports**. A country can import the natural resources that aren't available in its part of the world, as well as a wide range of products. And exports give countries and businesses more places to sell the natural resources they do have, as well as the products they make.

## WORDS TO KNOW!

**revenue:** money coming in.

**fee:** the cost of doing something.

**license:** permission to do something.

**tax:** money collected by the government to help it run.

**import:** any good or service that is brought in from another country.

**export:** any good or service that is shipped outside the country or brings in money from other countries.

Plants and animals are also considered natural resources. In the days before machines, places that were home to work animals—such as horses, oxen, camels, and elephants—had a big advantage over other parts of the world. And early societies that could grow corn, wheat, rice, and other grains that could feed lots of people and be stored for long periods were able to develop faster than areas where food had to be gathered every day. In the Middle Ages, countries in Asia and the Middle East became wealthy trading hard-to-find spices with Europe. Today, there is still worldwide trade in crops such as cotton, coffee, rubber, and wood.

*Plants and animals are* **renewable resources** *because we can raise new ones to replace the ones we used.*

## WORDS TO KNOW!

**renewable resource:** a resource that nature can replace.

**wind power:** electricity created by windmills turned by the wind.

**solar power:** electricity created by special panels that convert the energy of the sun.

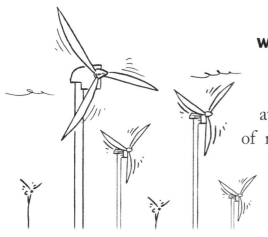

Some forms of energy, such as **wind power** and **solar power**, are also considered renewable. But even renewable resources must be handled carefully to avoid hurting the environment. As supplies of nonrenewable resources such as oil start to run out, governments are looking for ways to save natural resources for future generations.

# Inventing, Making, and Trading

An industry is made up of businesses that provide one kind of good or service. There are four main types.

- **Turning natural resources into raw materials that can be used by people and businesses.** Mining, farming, and oil companies are industries that fall into this category.

- **Manufacturing goods by hand or in factories.** These industries use raw materials to make everything from bread and dishes to cars and iPads.

- **Providing services.** Think of a plumber fixing broken pipes in your home, an artist doing the drawings for a comic book, or a doctor caring for sick patients at a hospital.

- **Conducting research and development.** Scientists and engineers come up with new ideas, new ways to do things, and new products.

**WORDS TO KNOW!**

**work force:** all the workers.

The kind of industry that develops in a country depends partly on its geography, history, and culture. A country must have the right ideas, the right raw materials and power, and the right **work force**.

## FASCINATING FACT

The Chinese were the first to make silk cloth from the cocoons of silkworms. They could do this because the worms, and the mulberry trees the silkworms feed on, were found there. Chinese families were given the job of raising silkworms in their homes. China led the silk market for centuries because they kept their knowledge of making silk a secret.

Britain was the center of the Industrial Revolution in the 1800s. It had vast deposits of coal, which could be burned for fuel, and iron ore, which could be made into metal tools and building materials. It also had colonies around the world that provided an additional source of raw materials. Inventors such as James Watt improved on ideas such as the steam engine, which could power machinery, trains, and ships. Many British workers moved to cities to work in the new factories and run the machines.

In the 1900s, the United States became the industrial leader of the world. Henry Ford created the car industry by making factories more efficient. Ray Kroc took that same idea to create McDonald's and launch the fast food industry. Meanwhile, new inventions such as television and computers kept U.S. industry growing. Today, the top spot in world industry goes to China. It too has lots of natural resources, and it also has an enormous work force willing to work for lower pay than workers in the United States. Today, Chinese factories make everything from processed food and toys to spacecraft.

Some micronations have their own industries. Collectors buy passports, coins, and paper money from micronations. At one point, the Northern Forest Archipelago in the Adirondack Mountains of New York had a web site that sold bumper stickers and garnets, a purple stone found in the region.

## FASCINATING FACT

Some micronations have a booming tourist industry. The Hutt River Province Principality in Australia welcomes busloads of tourists to stay in its campground and eat at its snack bar. The Conch Republic in Key West, Florida, draws visitors to its Independence Celebration every April with car races, pet shows, and a naval parade.

## Gross National Happiness

The gross domestic product (GDP) of a country is a measure of how many goods and services are produced each year. It is used to tell how well a country's economy is doing. Some people believe that the people in a country with a high GDP have a better life.

The country of Bhutan in the Himalaya Mountains looks at things differently. It measures how well it is doing with a gross national happiness (GNH) index. The GNH looks at the health of the people and the environment, rather than how much money its industries make. To increase GNH, Bhutan has promised to keep half its land covered in forest. And one day a month, it bans people from driving their cars, to cut down on air pollution.

The United Nations is looking at ways other countries can use Bhutan's GNH to improve quality of life around the world. How do you think the United States would rate on the GNH index? Can you think of other ways to measure a country's economic success?

## Money

The earliest economies didn't involve money at all. People **bartered** with each other to get the things they wanted. If a farmer had two cows and wanted some chickens, he would find a chicken farmer who wanted to trade.

*The problem with the bartering system was figuring out how many chickens equal one cow.*

### WORDS TO KNOW!

**barter:** to trade by exchanging one good or service for another.

Money was invented as a way to get around that problem. Instead of trading directly, people trade using coins or bills. **To be useful, money has to meet certain requirements.**

**It must be easy to carry around.** Cows are valuable, but they're hard to put in your pocket. Early forms of money included shells, beads, slabs of salt, and even the cacao beans used to make chocolate.

*In China, some of the first coins were made of metal and shaped like knives and garden tools.*

**It must come in small and large denominations.** If you buy a $2 candy bar with a $20 bill, you can get change using bills in denominations of $1, $2, $5, or $10. Long ago, people cut up coins like a pie into eight pieces. This is where the terms "pieces of eight" and "two bits" come from.

**It must be accepted by a large number of people.** Money is only useful if other people will take it as payment. Originally, money was made out of materials that were valuable in themselves, such as gold and silver. Paper was first used in China as a receipt to show that money was being held in the bank. It took centuries for people to trust paper money.

## FASCINATING FACT

Salt was used to pay soldiers in ancient Rome. That's where the word *salary* comes from, to describe a payment from an employer to a worker on a regular basis for doing a job!

*Whether it's made of gold, silver, or paper, money is only a symbol. It's valuable only when everyone agrees to treat it that way.*

The value of money can change when it is transferred from one country to another. The **exchange rate** between two countries depends on how each country's economy is doing. That's why sometimes the Canadian dollar is worth a little bit more than the American dollar and sometimes it's worth a little bit less.

## WORDS TO KNOW!

**exchange rate:** the value of one country's money in terms of another country's money.

**monetary system:** a country's laws and systems for controlling how money is made and used, including mints to print more money and banks to distribute it.

**community currency:** money that can only be used in the community that created it.

## Money from Micronations

Many micronations have their own currencies similar to regular money. The basic unit of currency in Molossia is the Valora, which is equal to 100 Futtrus. Three Valora are equal to the price in U.S. dollars of a tube of Pillsbury Cookie Dough. Why do you think they chose dough?

The Northern Forest Archipelago invented its own entire **monetary system**. One NFA Sweat Equity Buck is equal to one hour of work. King James III began the system by paying citizens who helped him build his nation's capital—the treehouse in his back yard. Then, those citizens use NFA bucks to buy things from stores owned by other NFA citizens. This type of monetary system is called **community currency**. It can only be used in the community that creates it.

Other community currencies in use around the United States include Davis Dollars in Davis, California; Cascadia Hours in Portland, Oregon; and LETS (Local Exchange Trading System) in Asheville, North Carolina.

# CREATE YOUR OWN
## Monetary System

A monetary system is more than just the bills and coins that a country uses for money. It involves the value of that money and how it is exchanged. Is a candy bar so valuable that it costs more than a pair of shoes? Does a babysitter earn more than a doctor? Use the questions below to help create your own monetary system. Then make your own bills and coins with the projects that follow.

### SUPPLIES

- ○ writing tools
- ○ paper

**1** What is the basic unit of currency in your country called?

**2** What is it worth? For example, what is the cost of items such as these?

* candy bar
* mailing a letter
* loaf of bread
* TV

* bicycle
* car
* house

**3** How much do these jobs pay, per hour or per year?

* babysitter
* pet store owner
* doctor
* police officer
* professional athlete

* movie star
* astronaut
* city mayor
* ruler

**4** What is the rate of exchange of your money with these other currencies?

* United State's dollar
* Canadian dollar
* Euro
* Valora

# MINT YOUR OWN
# Coins

Some countries such as Canada have replaced some paper bills with coins. These $1 and $2 coins are larger and have interesting designs, including a dinosaur. Polymer clay such as Sculpey is good for making coins because it bakes in a few minutes to a nice hard shape. You can find it in a variety of realistic metallic colors, or mix the color you like best. **Ask an adult for help when using the oven.**

**1** Soften the clay by handling it for a few minutes. Then press it flat with your hand or a rolling pin. Cut out some coin shapes using whatever tools you prefer.

**2** To make a mold for a raised design on your coin, take a sharp stick or plastic knife and draw the design on a foam plate. Remember that the final clay version will be the reverse of your mold! Press hard to make grooves in the foam.

**3** Press the clay coin into the mold, then pull it out carefully. Bake the clay according to the package directions to harden it.

**BUILD IT YOURSELF**

# MAKE YOUR OWN
## Counterfeit-Proof Paper Money

Many countries add security features to their paper money to prevent **counterfeiting**. What security features do you see on a $20 bill? The United States uses strips of reflective Mylar plastic and ink in different colors. Australian money is printed on plastic, and includes a clear window with stars printed on it. You can make your own money with your own security features. Look at real money or pictures of money from micronations for ideas on what to include on yours. Have fun!

**1** Design your paper money using symbols of your country. If you like, include a portrait of a famous person from your country's history—or yourself! Don't forget to write out the amount of the bill in the corners.

**2** Add a few hard-to-copy elements to protect your bills from counterfeiting. To make a rainbow-colored border or frame, hold three or more pens together while you draw a wavy outline around the edge of your money.

**3** A Mylar strip is also on real money to protect it from forgery. Cut a thin strip (or other shape) and glue it onto your design.

**4** Some bills have secret designs that can only be seen under **ultraviolet light**, also called black light. To make your own, soak out the ink from a highlighter by swishing around the felt tip in a cup of water. Now use the marker to draw a secret design right over the regular ink. It should be almost invisible until you hold it up to a black lightbulb. For best results, use paper the same color as your highlighter.

# CHAPTER FIVE

# All Systems Go—Your Country's Infrastructure

**WHO BUILDS AND MAINTAINS ROADS AND BRIDGES**
so that people and goods can move from one place to another?
Who delivers the mail or builds a network of telephone lines
that carry Internet and phone services? How do you get
water? Systems and infrastructure tie a country together,
keep it safe, and help people get the things they need. Your
country needs systems and infrastructure to function.

# Transportation

The saying "All roads lead to Rome" explains how the Roman Empire was able to conquer Europe. More than 2,000 years ago, the Romans developed a vast network of roads across the continent. Much of this transportation system was paved, making it easier and faster for people on horseback and in horse-drawn carts to travel. Their transportation system enabled the Romans to send soldiers, supplies, and goods back and forth between the capital and the farthest reaches of the empire. Centuries later, new ideas and inventions spread from Asia to the Middle East and Europe along that same network of roads.

In the United States, transportation systems helped the country grow rapidly from a small group of colonies into a modern superpower. **Several systems made this possible.**

**Canals and waterways:** When Europeans first moved to North America, the continent did not have a system of roads. The first cities developed on the coast and along rivers, where ships and barges could easily carry people and materials. In the 1800s, the government began building canals to connect waterways. With the opening of the Erie Canal in New York State, boats could get to the Midwest from New York City. The Panama Canal, built by the United States across a narrow strip of Central America, connected the Atlantic Ocean to the Pacific Ocean in 1914.

*Using the canal, people could get to the West Coast without having to make a difficult and dangerous land crossing.*

**Trains:** By the mid-1800s, steam engines made travel over land even quicker. But it meant building hundreds of miles of railway to carry them. So the federal government passed a law authorizing the construction of the Transcontinental Railroad. Two companies, the Central Pacific and the Union Pacific, began laying track to extend train lines in the East to the Pacific Coast. The companies started at each end and met in the middle in Promontory, Utah.

## FASCINATING FACT

The micronation of Molossia in Nevada opened its own railroad line in March 2000. The model railroad, with the motto, "Serving Molossia for over a tenth of a century," is too small to actually ride in, however.

*When the line was completed in 1869, it cut the trip cross-country from four months to less than four days.*

## Public Versus Private

In the United States, many of the earliest highways were private **turnpikes**. Travelers had to pay the owner a toll to use the road. Today, the government owns most roads, but bus and railroad lines are still often privately owned. In other countries, the government runs nearly all forms of **mass transit**.

Because private companies compete with each other for business, they don't like to work together. This can create problems, such as the lack of connections between private subway lines in New York City in the early 1900s. Today, the same kinds of problems are seen with cell phone companies, which are all competing to have cell phone towers that give customers the best coverage.

## WORDS TO KNOW!

**turnpike:** a major road that you pay to use.

**mass transit:** a system for moving large numbers of people on buses, trains, or other vehicles.

**Cars:** The invention of the gas-powered automobile created the need for a whole new transportation network. Car owners wanted paved roads that let them drive from their homes to where they worked and shopped. Soon they wanted to take their cars on longer trips, too. In the 1950s, the U.S. government built the Interstate Highway System to connect cities across the entire country with faster, wider roads. The highways helped industries expand by giving them an easy way to truck goods from one end of the country to the other.

## FASCINATING FACT

The U.S. Interstate Highway System is also known as the Dwight D. Eisenhower National System of Interstate and Defense Highways. Its original purpose was the same as the Roman military roads—to help move armies quickly in case of attack.

**Planes:** In the 1900s, air travel cut the time needed to cross the continent from a few days to just a few hours. That required yet another new system. Airports were built and an air traffic control system helped airplanes operate safely and efficiently.

# Communication

If transportation moves people and goods, then communication moves information. For most of human history, the most reliable way to send messages was by hand or by mouth. So better transportation was the key to better communication. The earliest communication network was a string of outposts along a road, each with a messenger ready to go. When government officials needed to send a message, a runner or messenger on horseback carried it to the nearest outpost. From there, a new messenger would take it to the next outpost along the route. This continued until the message reached its destination.

## Report Card on America's Infrastructure

There's more to developing a country's infrastructure than building roads and communications systems. You also need to keep them in tip-top shape. When the infrastructure in a country doesn't get the attention it needs, the whole country can start to fall apart, literally. In 2009, the Lake Champlain Bridge between Crown Point, New York, and Addison, Vermont, had to be dynamited and replaced because engineers feared it was about to collapse from cracks in the 80-year-old concrete. Every year, the American Society of Civil Engineers issues its Report Card on America's Infrastructure. In 2013, the report said that bumps and holes in the nation's roads cost the average driver more than $300 a year in extra repairs.

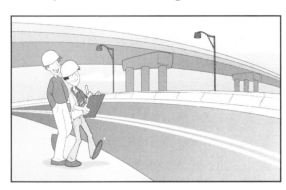

In ancient Persia, in what is now Iran, King Darius had a famous staff of swift riders who could carry a message the length of his realm along the Persian Royal Road in only days. The Inca Empire of South America built tens of thousands of miles of trails through the Andes Mountains for its messengers on foot. In the United States, the Pony Express only operated from 1860 to 1861, but it cut down the time to carry a message across the country to 10 days. Pony Express riders traveled between stations set 10 miles (16 kilometers) apart.

Even in early times there were some crude ways used to send signals over long distances. Some countries lit flames to send signals to ships at sea or to message stations set within sight of each other. Mirrors were also used to signal on sunny days. The ancient Greeks were the first to train homing pigeons to fly to their starting points carrying written messages. And Native Americans used smoke signals.

The **telegraph** was the first device to use electricity to send messages. In the mid-1800s, telegraph wires were strung along railroad lines. Cables were even laid across the ocean floor between the United States and Europe. People used a local telegraph

## WORDS TO KNOW!

**telegraph:** a device for tapping out coded messages over wires using electrical signals.

office to send or receive messages in Morse code, an alphabet of short and long signals called dots and dashes. The telephone used the same kind of system of wires but allowed people to talk to each other directly.

*Soon companies were building telephone lines to houses and businesses, creating an enormous communications network.*

Today, a large portion of communication happens over the airwaves. Radio and television companies send out signals using a network of towers on the ground and satellites circling above the earth. But the biggest advance in communication has been the use of cell phones and devices that access the Internet. Using satellites and cell phone towers, anyone with a device can share information around the country and around the world in an instant.

# Power of the Press

Before the invention of the **printing press**, it was hard for one person, even a ruler, to send a message to everyone in the country. But once printing arrived, anyone could produce hundreds or thousands of copies of a book, newspaper, magazine, or poster. The press became a powerful way for ordinary citizens to spread news and information about how a country was being run. That made freedom of the press an important right in a democracy. Private **media** companies competed for customers by building a reputation for presenting the news accurately. When a ruler or government wanted to keep tight control of the people, one of the first things it did was take over the news media. Today, anyone can transmit news and information using the Internet. This can cause problems because it can be hard to tell if an individual is being accurate. But videos and reports people send live from the scene on web sites such as YouTube, Facebook, and Twitter have become useful tools for gathering news. In Egypt in 2012, citizens used the Internet to share information and band together to fight for change and overthrow the government.

## WORDS TO KNOW!

**printing press:** a machine that prints multiple copies of a document.

**media:** the industry in the business of presenting news to the public, by methods including radio, television, Internet, and newspapers.

# You've Got Mail: The Postal System

Mail is a way to send a private message to just one person. The first letters didn't use stamps. If you got a letter, you had to pay to receive it. But rates were so high many people looked for a way to get out of paying. They wrote messages in a secret code on the outside of the letter. The person who got the letter could read the code without paying for and opening the letter. The first postage stamp was issued in Britain in 1840 as a way to make sure people paid to read their mail!

Originally, most stamps showed a portrait of a famous ruler. But from the beginning, countries also made decorative stamps. Stamps can be very colorful and feature beautiful paintings of people or scenes. In fact, some small countries issue stamps with fun or lovely designs to raise money by selling them to collectors, just as some micronations do! You can find stamps with pictures of anything from toys or cartoon characters to famous rock stars.

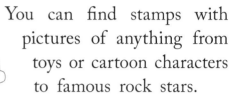

The postal service is the government agency that distributes the mail. Mail carriers pick up letters at your home, bring them to the post office for sorting, and then deliver them to the addresses you put on the envelopes. However, compared to email, that system is slow and expensive. Between email and private mail companies that compete with the government postal service, the U.S. Postal Service has lost a lot of business.

Many micronations issue their own stamps, and the Northern Forest Archipelago also created its own postal service. Citizens could drop a stamped envelope into a nearby Postal Delivery Receptacle (PDR), which was a small metal container found in the NFA capital and other locations. As citizens traveled around the micronation, they were encouraged to check PDRs to see if there was mail addressed to their next destinations. When the mail was delivered, the carrier took the used envelope to any government office to be paid with stamps.

# More Systems and Infrastructure

**Water:** Some of the earliest forms of infrastructure were **aqueducts** and **irrigation** systems to provide water for drinking and farming. There are cities in desert regions in Europe, Asia, and the Middle East that still use underground water systems built more than a thousand years ago. Some cities in the United States today get their water from far-away **reservoirs**. The pipelines carrying that water, and the systems to treat and filter the water to make sure it is clean enough to drink, are an important piece of a country's infrastructure.

> **WORDS TO KNOW!**
>
> **aqueduct:** a network of channels used to direct water over long distances from its source to where it will be used.
>
> **irrigation:** a system of ditches to transport water through farmland.
>
> **reservoir:** a man-made or natural lake used to store water for drinking and other uses.
>
> **vaccine:** medicine designed to keep a person from getting a particular disease, usually given by needle.
>
> **anesthesia:** medicine used during an operation to put patients to sleep and keep them from feeling pain.

*Dealing with solid and liquid waste has always been a big infrastructure challenge. The first city sewer systems to carry away waste from toilets date back to the ancient Romans.*

**Health Care:** From ancient times until the end of the 1800s, most people took care of their own health using homemade remedies. Doctors had some idea of how the body worked, but there was very little they could do to treat most diseases. The development of **vaccines** and **anesthesia** changed all that.

Today's health care system includes hospitals and clinics, as well as the doctors, emergency medical technicians, and other health care workers who staff them. In the United States, the health care system is mostly privately owned and run. Almost all other countries in the world provide health care for all citizens through the government. **Some of the other health needs that are usually handled by the government include:**

- protecting citizens from outbreaks of infectious diseases such as the flu through **public health** departments;

- **regulating** food and medicine to be sure they are safe; and

- making and enforcing safety rules about things we use in our homes and workplaces, such as tools, cars, and toys.

> ### WORDS TO KNOW!
>
> **public health:** a system that works to keep the population as a whole healthy.
>
> **regulate:** to control something with laws and supervision.

**Energy:** Whether public or privately owned, countries today need systems to produce electricity and fuel and send it to the places it is needed. What are the different pieces of the energy infrastructure?

- power plants fueled by coal

- hydroelectric plants fueled by running water

- wind turbine farms fueled by the wind

- solar panels fueled by the sun

- refineries that process oil

- oil and gas wells to collect oil and gas from underground

Our energy infrastructure also includes all the power lines and pipelines that carry electricity and fuel from where it is made or processed to storage facilities, homes, and businesses.

## Blackouts

Power grids are networks of wires that connect systems in different areas. They are used to send electricity from one place to another when needed. But all that connectedness can spell trouble. In 2003, the biggest blackout in United States history began when some tree branches touched a power line in Ohio. The blackout spread from New York City to Canada. More than 50 million people went without electricity for as long as two days before it was fixed!

**Safety:** Fire and police protection are part of the safety infrastructure provided by local governments. At the national level, there are courts and prisons to deal with serious crimes or those that involve more than one state. The national government is also in charge of coordinating fire, police, and other safety personnel to help with natural disasters such as earthquakes and hurricanes.

**Security:** A country's security infrastructure protects its people from threats inside and outside its borders. To guard against attack, a country may need military bases, ships, tanks, aircraft, and weapon storage facilities. At border crossings, government workers check people and goods to make sure nothing illegal is brought into the country.

## FASCINATING FACT

Countries throughout history have built walls along their borders to keep out invaders or keep their own people in. The Great Wall of China was created as protection against neighboring tribes. After World War II, the communist government in East Germany put up the Berlin Wall to prevent citizens from fleeing to West Germany, which was democratic. In 2006, the United States began building a fence on its border with Mexico to stop people from crossing illegally. Do you think this fence has been a success or a failure? Would you welcome new citizens into your micronation or try to keep people from joining?

# Schools

The idea of a public school system is relatively new in history. The first teachers were parents. Wealthy families hired **tutors** or sent their children to private schools. To learn particular skills, such as medicine or law, young adults attended universities where they studied with experts. To learn a skilled craft, a position as an **apprentice** with a weaver, **cobbler**, or printer, for example, led to a job in that area. Religious institutions such as churches also provided a source of education. Religious leaders were often the most educated people in a community.

## WORDS TO KNOW!

**tutor:** a teacher who works with only one student, often privately in the student's home.

**apprentice:** a person who learns a job or skill by working for someone who is good at it.

**cobbler:** a person who makes shoes.

## Try This! Teach Children About Your Country

Too many kids think social studies is boring. Your job is to make up a lesson that teaches kids all about your amazing micronation—but make sure it won't put anyone to sleep! What are some ways to do that? You could make your country sound like an incredible place to live by describing all the things you like about it. You can make up puzzles and games for kids to play to learn the names and fun facts about your micronation. What does your country look like? How do the people who live there spend their day? Are there any interesting plants or animals? Unusual customs, foods, or traditions? You can even make a short movie showing kids what a typical day in your country is like. What are some other ways to make kids excited to learn about different countries?

## WORDS TO KNOW!

**homeschool:** to teach children at home, usually done by the parents.

**nonprofit:** an organization supported by donations whose main mission is to help people, animals, the environment, or other causes.

Governments around the world began to create public school systems in the late 1800s. Laws requiring education between certain ages made sure that families sent their children. Most children attend public school in the United States, but many go to private schools.

*There are also a growing number of families who teach their children at home using public school programs or who* **homeschool** *on their own.*

The education system can also include things such as museums, libraries, research centers, and laboratories. Some are publicly owned and some are **nonprofit** organizations.

## FASCINATING FACT

You might like the school system in Finland, where children don't begin school until age 7 and there's no homework or testing until high school. Students in Finland rank highest in the world in math, science, and reading. Students in the United States rank 15th or lower in the same subjects.

# The Department of
# Weights and Measures

It helps when everyone in a country measures things in the same way. Every major country in history has adopted standards of measurement. The Egyptians and the Greeks had official weights and measures that every **merchant** and builder had to match.

*In the 1300s, England declared an "inch" to be the length of three barleycorns laid end to end. A "yard" was defined as the length of King Edward III's arm.*

## WORDS TO KNOW!

**merchant:** someone who buys and sells goods for profit.

**metric system:** a system of weights and measures based on the number 10.

In the 1700s, French scientists created the **metric system** based on a fraction of the distance between the equator and the North Pole. Most of the world—except for the United States—has made the metric system its main system of measurement.

## FASCINATING FACT

In 2002, the dictator of Turkmenistan in Central Asia changed the calendar for his country. He renamed the month of January after himself, and the month of April after his mother. The names were changed back after the dictator's death in 2008.

Besides length, width, height, and weight, what else do countries measure? One thing is time. The ancient Romans rearranged the calendar to create new months for their rulers. The months of July and August were named for the emperors Julius Caesar and Augustus Caesar.

Micronations can choose any measurement system or create an entirely new one. The Northern Forest Archipelago created NFAST, which stood for Northern Forest Archipelago Standard Time. It's like a metric system for clocks. A day was broken up into 10,000 units of time called the *tic*, defined as the amount of time it takes to drink a glass of water without rushing. Other units were the *toc* (the time it takes an adult to walk 100 meters on a trail in the NFA capital), *tac* (the amount of time it takes to start a fire in a fireplace), and *tuc* (the time it takes to make, eat, and clean up a meal with friends). Breakfast time in the NFA was at 2,500, lunchtime was at 5,000, and dinner was at 7,500.

The Republic of Molossia has its own time zone, Molossian Standard Time, which is 39 minutes ahead of Pacific Standard Time and 21 minutes behind Mountain Standard Time. Length is measured in Nortons. A Norton is equal to 7 inches (17.7 centimeters), the length of the president's hand. The Molossian unit of weight is the Fenwick, which is equal to 2 pounds (0.9 kilogram), the weight of one large tube of Pillsbury Cookie Dough.

## Try This! Design a System of Measurement

Your micronation can have its own system of measurements! First, you need to decide what standard you will use to measure things against. Then, come up with some names for the different units (small, medium, and large). Now, design your own calendar. You can rearrange the calendar to suit your needs as well. Add another month to summer to make vacation last longer or make four-day weekends every month. Why not? It's up to you!

# BUILD YOUR OWN
## Model Landmark to Scale

When tourists visit a foreign country, they often go to the wondrous buildings and structures there. In Paris, it is the Eiffel Tower. In Egypt, the pyramids. New York has the Empire State Building and San Francisco has the Golden Gate Bridge. In China, they walk along the Great Wall.

## WORDS TO KNOW!

**scale:** the size of a map, model, drawing, or diagram compared to the actual object, shown as two measurements in relation to one another, such as "1 inch to 3 miles" or 1:3.

**dimension:** the size of something given as a measurement, such as "1 foot high."

## SUPPLIES

- graph paper
- pens or pencils
- ruler
- building materials such as building block toys, toothpicks and gumdrops, empty paper towel rolls or rolled up newspaper, folded origami paper or cardstock, cardboard boxes and duct tape, papier mâché, clay or modeling dough, sticks and twine, milk jugs and other recycled materials

Some fans of famous buildings like to create models to **scale** using wood, plastic, or other materials. One artist has built models of world landmarks using nothing but toothpicks and glue! Here's how to create a scale model of a famous landmark from your micronation. Whether it is a building, bridge, or giant spaceship, you can get as creative as you want with the materials.

**1** Find a photograph of the landmark you want to build to use as a guide, or make a rough sketch if you are creating your own. You will also need to know how high it is at its tallest point.

**2** Before you build your scale model, it helps to draw a diagram. To make things simple, just show the front. Graph paper makes it easy to measure your drawing—just count how many boxes there are on each side. Use a ruler to make the lines straight. Start by drawing a straight line to show the bottom of your landmark. Make sure your whole drawing will fit on the paper! If the object is wider than it is tall, turn the paper sideways.

BUILD IT YOURSELF

**3** Now figure out how tall your drawing should be. Pick a number of boxes that is easy to work with, such as 10 or 20 boxes high. Mark it on the graph paper, then fill in the rest of the drawing. You don't need to know the measurement of each part. Just compare each side to the total height. For instance, if the building is 20 boxes high and it's roughly twice as high as it is wide, make your drawing 10 boxes wide. Be sure to write the number of boxes along each side.

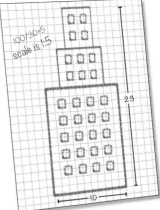

**4** Put the scale on your drawing, so anyone looking at it will know how big the actual landmark is. The scale tells you one box is equal to a certain number of feet or meters. To find the scale, divide the height of the actual landmark by the number of boxes in the drawing. If your drawing is 20 boxes high and the actual landmark is 20 feet tall, your scale is one to one—one box equals 1 foot. But if the landmark is 40 feet high, then each box has to represent 2 feet, so your scale is one to two (written as 1:2).

**5** Before you can build your model, you need to figure out a new scale. Decide how high your model will be in inches or centimeters, then divide the height of the model by the number of boxes in the diagram. So if your diagram is 20 boxes high and your model is 60 inches high, divide 60 by 20 to get 3. One box = 3 inches, so the new scale is 1:3.

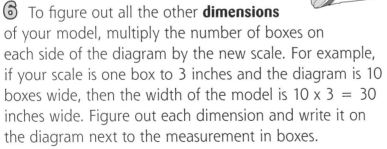

**6** To figure out all the other **dimensions** of your model, multiply the number of boxes on each side of the diagram by the new scale. For example, if your scale is one box to 3 inches and the diagram is 10 boxes wide, then the width of the model is 10 x 3 = 30 inches wide. Figure out each dimension and write it on the diagram next to the measurement in boxes.

**7** With your diagram, the new dimensions, and a ruler, measure out your building materials. When you are finished, your model should look like the diagram and also be a pretty good copy of your landmark!

# MAKE YOUR OWN
## Disaster Movie!

Your micronation needs a plan in case of natural disaster or attack from other nations, species, or planets. Think about a disaster that might strike your country. Then come up with a story that shows how your emergency services and defense forces would handle it.

**SUPPLIES**

- ⦿ paper
- ⦿ pen or pencil
- ⦿ ruler
- ⦿ video camera or smart phone

**1** Write a script that tells what happens in your movie. Give your characters names that fit their personalities and backgrounds. It should have dialogue—the words each character says—and a description of what they are doing. To make it easy to read, start a new line every time a new person speaks, like this:

★ **Joe:** (pointing) Oh no, that alien ship is heading right for the city!

★ **Jane:** Quick, call the National Space Patrol!

**2** Make a storyboard to show what happens in each scene. A storyboard looks like the panels of a comic book. Take a piece of paper and hold it sideways, so it is wider than it is high. Draw a line dividing it in half from top to bottom and another line dividing it in half from side to side to create four boxes. Draw one scene from the movie in each box, showing the background, characters, and any special effects.

**3** How are you going to create your movie? You can make a live-action video starring you and your friends or use action figures against a background you create (look up techniques for stop-motion animation). Or you can draw the whole thing by hand or on your computer and use an animation program to make it move. Good luck and have fun!

**BUILD IT YOURSELF**

# MAKE YOUR OWN
## Stamps

To make some stamps for your micronation, first take a look at real stamps and stamps from other micronations for inspiration. You can display them as a sheet or stick them on envelopes.

## SUPPLIES

- ○ peel-and-stick labels (or plain paper and glue)
- ○ colored pens
- ○ mailing envelope

**1** What shape do you want to make your stamps? You can choose anything! Draw the outline of the shape on your label paper. If you want to make several stamps, repeat the shape several times.

**2** Inside the stamp, draw the image you want to use. It can be the face of your micronation's leader or another famous person. You can also use any of your country's symbols, such as the official animal or a landmark building. The value of the stamp in your nation's currency should also be shown, usually as a small number in a corner of the stamp.

## FASCINATING FACT

When email first became popular, some people started using the phrase "snail mail" to refer to paper messages sent in envelopes.

**3** If you like, cut out your stamp and place it on an envelope, ready to be mailed. You can also design a decorative cancellation mark to make the

stamp look used. A cancellation is an ink mark placed with a rubber stamp over the postage stamp and the envelope to show it has been used. A simple cancellation is a circular postmark with the date and place, plus wavy bars or lines. Cancellations for special occasions can show scenes or carry messages.

**BUILD IT YOURSELF**

# CHAPTER SIX

## Cultural Geography—Forge Your Own National Identity

**HOW DOES CULTURE CONNECT INDIVIDUALS AND BUILD** loyalty to a nation? It is one of the main things that makes a country unique. The culture of a place tells you something about its physical environment, its economy, and the values of the people who live there. Culture is expressed by the food people eat, the clothes they wear, and the homes they share with their families. A country's culture may include its own language, holidays, games, art, music, and stories. All of these things make people feel connected to their country.

*When all the citizens in a country share the same culture, it can make it easier for everyone to understand each other.*

But a country with people who come from different cultures has advantages too. It can draw on different ideas and traditions and find more ways to connect with people around the world. People who share a culture can still feel a part of a place even when they live in a different country. Your micronation doesn't require a physical location to create a culture that all your citizens share.

## National Holidays

Every country has national holidays held in honor of famous people and events in its history. New countries usually celebrate their Independence Day with **patriotic** displays. In the United States, Americans toast the publication of the Declaration of Independence on July 4, 1776, with parades and fireworks. India's Independence Day happened on August 15, 1947, when the British returned rule to the Indian people. Their celebration involves speeches and flying kites in their flag's colors of orange, white, and green.

## WORDS TO KNOW!

**patriotic:** showing love for your country.

## FASCINATING FACT

John Adams, the second president of the United States, was the first to suggest fireworks on the Fourth of July. "It ought to be solemnized with Pomp and Parade, with Shows, Games, Sports, Guns, Bells, Bonfires and Illuminations from one End of this Continent to the other from this Time forward forever more," he wrote to his wife, Abigail, on July 3, 1776. It wasn't until 1941, however, that Independence Day became an official national holiday.

Some countries have national holidays that focus on families. Coming of Age Day is a Japanese holiday that dates back more than a thousand years. On the second Monday in January, everyone who will turn 20 years old that year becomes an official adult on that day. They dress up in formal clothing and go to local government offices to hear speeches and receive small gifts. Japan also has a Children's Day with martial arts demonstrations, singing, and plays performed by children.

## FASCINATING FACT

Some national holidays are more serious. Armistice Day began as a solemn event to mark the end of World War I on November 11, 1918. Today, the holiday is called Veterans Day and honors everyone who served in the military.

In the United States, Thanksgiving Day means a big family feast of turkey, cranberries, and pumpkin pie. The first Thanksgiving was a dinner held in 1621 by English settlers to thank the Native Americans who helped them when they first arrived.

Micronations have holidays too. Every year on January 8, Molossia celebrates Emperor Norton I Day. It is named after Joshua Abraham Norton, the **patron saint** of unrecognized nations. Norton was a businessman who struck it rich during the Gold Rush of the 1850s in San Francisco. But he later lost his fortune and disappeared for several years. When he returned, he proclaimed himself Norton I, Emperor of these United States and Protector of Mexico.

## WORDS TO KNOW!

**patron saint:** a person from history, legend, or religious tradition who is looked up to as a hero or protector for a particular group of people.

Norton could often be seen roaming the streets in his military uniform, carrying his sword. He even printed up his own money. The people of San Francisco treated Norton with respect. He was given the best seats at plays and concerts and marched at the head of parades. When he died in 1880, flags were lowered and businesses closed. More than 20,000 people attended his funeral. Norton Day is celebrated in Molossia with a meal of San Francisco–inspired food. There is also a Cookie Dough Fest, where citizens eat raw cookie dough—the basis of Molossia's monetary system— and watch scary movies. What special holidays will you create for your micronation? Are there any people or events you want to honor?

# Holidays in the Aerican Empire

The micronation of Aerica has several unique holidays on its calendar. This is just a sampling.

- ☉ **February 27, \*Oops\* Day:** Commemorating the day the Tower of Pisa in Italy became the Leaning Tower of Pisa.

- ☉ **June 2, Important People Day:** A day to celebrate important people who don't have their own day.

- ☉ **October 12, International Moment of Frustration Scream Day:** At noon, people are encouraged to go outside and have a nice scream about whatever's bothering them.

- ☉ **December 23, Happy Things Day:** A day in honor of any happy things that took place in the past year.

## Try This! Show Off Your Micronation's Most Important Holiday

Write a news report or film a news segment describing how your micronation celebrates an important national holiday. Your report can cover:

- ❂ the history or event that led to the creation of the holiday
- ❂ any ceremonies that are held
- ❂ traditional songs, dances, or games that take place
- ❂ any special costumes people wear
- ❂ what people like to eat on this important day

## Food

Food is a big part of a country's culture. As with other things people associate with a particular country, a country's traditional **cuisine** can be traced to its location and environment. Tropical countries where pineapples, oranges, and bananas are found will enjoy a large selection of fruit. Places that are good for growing wheat, rice, or corn will have more bread and other grains in the diet. And countries with a cold climate and a short growing season will have fewer plants to eat and rely more on meat and milk.

> # WORDS TO KNOW!
>
> **cuisine:** food that is cooked in a particular way or food that a country is known for.

*Cuisines also vary by taste. Some countries, such as Mexico and India, are known for their spicy food. Different cultures also have different ideas of a favorite delicacy.*

In Korea, sea slugs are considered a treat. In the Philippines, people like purple yam ice cream. In Poland, they eat chilled jellied cow foot with horseradish. Food is so important to a people's identity that when they move to a different country they take their food traditions with them.

We think of some foods as belonging to a particular culture. But many people enjoy trying new foods and it's common for countries to adopt food from other places. Sometimes it's even hard to guess where a food came from. Hamburgers and hot dogs, also known as frankfurters, are as American as the Fourth of July. But only the bun is native to the United States. The original meat dishes came from the German cities of Hamburg and Frankfurt. Yogurt is a popular snack, but it goes back to Asian desert herders who needed a way to preserve milk without refrigeration. And Switzerland is famous for its chocolate. But it was unknown in Europe until explorers brought it there from Mexico, where the ancient Maya and Aztecs thought it had magical properties.

## WORDS TO KNOW!

**Silk Road:** the ancient network of trade routes connecting the Mediterranean Sea and China by land.

## FASCINATING FACT

If you think spaghetti and tomato sauce is a native Italian dish, think again! Noodles were invented in Central Asia and introduced to Italy by merchants who discovered it while traveling along the **Silk Road**. And the tomato plant originally came from South America. It wasn't introduced to Europe until Spanish explorers brought it back from the New World in the 1500s.

## Try This! Make a Locavore Meal

Want to get a taste of the geography of food? Try being a **locavore**! See if you can create a meal using only ingredients that come from within your state or province. You can find food at local farms, farmer's markets, in your garden, even in your back yard! In many cultures, weeds such as dandelion leaves are considered delicacies. Some cultures eat insects, frogs, and other small animals, although you may not want to go that far. You should always get adult permission before eating anything you find in the wild. If there are bakeries or other food companies in your area, ask if they have an outlet store or give tours.

### WORDS TO KNOW!

**locavore:** a person who makes an effort to eat food that is grown close by.

**status:** the position of someone in a group.

## Clothing

Traditionally, styles of clothing were based mainly on the surrounding geography and culture. In warm climates, people can wear less than in chillier regions. People who do rough work need sturdier clothes than those who stay clean indoors most of the time. Clothes and jewelry are also a way to show your **status** in society. Clothing made of fine silk is a sign that the wearer is wealthy and has servants to cook and clean.

*Many countries and cultures have their own traditional clothing, sometimes called a national costume.*

## FASCINATING FACT

Kids often have their own food culture different from adults. That's because our tastes change as we get older. Young children have a strong liking for sweets, while older adults often find a bitter taste such as coffee more interesting. An experiment to see what kids would pick from a school salad bar showed other differences—the students chose bread cubes over lettuce and they liked to keep all the ingredients in separate piles.

Today, people may only wear traditional clothing on special occasions, but it's still a way to identify where a person is from. The sari is a type of dress from India, for example. It consists of a long piece of cloth that is wrapped around the body many times. A kimono is the traditional costume of Japan. It resembles a robe, with an elaborate belt around the waist. In the Middle East, a long, loose robe called a caftan is a traditional way of keeping cool in a hot climate. The traditional outfit of people living near the Arctic Circle includes a fur parka and warm boots.

Most countries also have official uniforms that indicate special jobs. You can identify members of the police, fire, or military by their uniforms. Mail carriers and hospital workers often have special uniforms too. And as mentioned before, uniforms and other clothing items can be symbols of power, to show that the wearer is a member of the ruling class. Even colors can indicate where you stand in society. The dye used to make clothing purple, for instance, used to be so rare and expensive it was only worn by royalty. The dye could only be made from a special kind of sea snail.

## WORDS TO KNOW!

**dialect:** a form of a language used by people in one area.

**accent:** a particular way of saying words, usually used by people from one area.

## Language

People started using spoken language and sign language at least 100,000 years ago. At one time there were as many as 15,000 different languages around the world. Today, there are between 5,000 and 6,000. People are often proud of their native languages. Every language can claim its own poetry, stories, and traditions.

Hi!

Hey.

Hello.

Even though languages can tie people together, sometimes people who speak the same language can sound very different. Americans sometimes have a hard time understanding people from Australia or Scotland, even though they all speak English. And even one country can have different **dialects** and **accents**. That's why Southerners sound so different from people from New Jersey.

Some different languages sound very similar. In fact, some languages are so similar that people from one country can talk to people from another country without too much trouble. For instance, people who live in The Netherlands speak Dutch. People who live in Germany speak German. But along the border between the two countries, the languages sound very much alike.

*Languages are changing all the time. As people from one region come into contact with people from another, they borrow words from each other.*

Most languages can be traced back to only a few different language families. English has roots in both German and French, because people from those cultures invaded England at different times. French in turn belongs to the Romance language family, which traces its roots back to Latin, the language of the Roman Empire.

## Cu Vi Parolas Esperanton? (Do You Speak Esperanto?)

Esperanto is a language invented in 1887 by an eye doctor named L.L. Zamenhof. He lived in the Polish city of Bialystok, where many different languages were spoken. He created Esperanto so that more people could understand each other. The language uses only one sound for each letter, so it's easy to learn and to spell. And since its roots are based on Latin, English, German, Polish, and Russian, it is already similar to many languages. It is estimated that about a million people around the world use Esperanto to read, write, and for fun.

The more people interact, the more their languages become alike. Because people need to speak a language that everyone can understand, less popular languages are disappearing. In China, people once spoke many different dialects of Chinese. Today, most people speak one dialect, Mandarin. English is the language heard most often on TV and in movies. It is often the language used when companies and governments work together. So other countries have begun to borrow English words in place of their own.

Not all countries are happy with this development. The French Academy is a government agency in France. Its job is to keep the French language pure. The Academy is always fighting the use of *franglais*. These are words that are a little bit English and a little bit French—like *le week-end*, *le talkie-walkie*, and *le shampooing*. Instead, the Academy has come up with new French words for new inventions. So the French word for "computer" is *l'ordinateur* and the word for "software" is *le logiciel*.

## Sports

Baseball is the national pastime in the United States. Canadians love hockey. Around the world, soccer is the number one sport. And micronations have their own sports, too. In Aerica they play Sillyball, a game involving "taunts, riddles, insults, and generally distracting mockery." Citizens of the Principality of Hutt River in Australia have competed around the world in the sports of Wife Carrying and Bog Snorkeling. In January 2013, Dame Julia Galvin represented the PHR at the Christmas Tree Throwing Competition in County Clare, Ireland.

# MAKE YOUR OWN
## Thrift-Shop Uniform

Part of inventing your own country is creating your own artifacts. The President of Molossia, Kevin Baugh, always advises new micronational leaders to make their own uniforms. His Excellency creates his own presidential uniform from used clothing he buys at thrift shops and online. His officer's cap is really an old police cap with gold fig leaves attached to the brim. His medals come from eBay. Baugh advises young micronationalists to put together their own uniforms, too. "Definitely do it on a shoestring," says the micronation expert. "It's more fun and way more impressive." Here are some tips for making your own wardrobe.

**1** Find clothing you can use to build your uniform by asking family and friends for hand-me-downs. You can also look at yard sales and online. Thrift stores often have formal wear for sale in the spring, around prom and wedding season. Look for suits, jackets, tuxedos, military uniforms, gowns, and other types of clothes usually worn on special occasions.

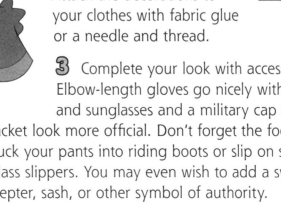

**2** Next, dress up your outfit with decorations. You can find them in sewing and department stores. Look for decorations used for curtains as well as for clothes. Attach the decorations to your clothes with fabric glue or a needle and thread.

**3** Complete your look with accessories. Elbow-length gloves go nicely with gowns, and sunglasses and a military cap make a jacket look more official. Don't forget the footwear! Tuck your pants into riding boots or slip on some glass slippers. You may even wish to add a sword, scepter, sash, or other symbol of authority.

## SUPPLIES

- old clothes, especially suits, gowns, and other formal wear
- decoration and trim, including fancy buttons, braiding, tassels, and sequins
- fabric glue or needle and thread
- accessories, including pins, neck chains, gloves, sun glasses, medals, tiaras, crowns, military caps, top hats, or other head coverings
- footwear, such as riding boots or high heels

**BUILD IT YOURSELF**

# INVENT YOUR OWN
# Language

Some micronations have their own languages to set them apart from the rest of the world. Aerica has several words of its own, including *smoo* (trouble), *soussan* (Are you okay), and *velcom* (I express joy at seeing you). Here are some ideas to help you invent a unique language for your micronation.

**1 Create a dialect:** Take standard English, put a twist on it, and you've got your own dialect. You probably know a few versions already. **Pidgin** English is a very simple mixture of English and words from other languages. It can sound a lot like baby talk: "Me want go zoo manana (tomorrow)." Pidgin languages evolved over time between people who spoke different languages so they could talk to each other, such as when traders or explorers first arrived in a new country.

## WORDS TO KNOW!

**pidgin:** a simple form of a language used to help people who speak different languages do business together.

**Pig Latin:** a play language formed by moving the sounds around in words.

**consonant:** sounds made by letters that are not vowels (a, e, i, o, and u).

**vowel:** the sounds made by the letters a, e, i, o, and u.

**inflection:** a rise or fall in the sound of a person's voice.

## FASCINATING FACT

Another English dialect, **Pig Latin**, is a code to keep secrets. To translate a word into Pig Latin, put the beginning **consonant** sound at the end and add "ay" to it: "Aylor-Tay ent-way ast-fay." Another version, Ubbi Dubbi, which puts "ub" in front of every **vowel**, was made popular by the kids' TV show *ZOOM*. You can create your own code by placing an extra sound in the beginning, middle, or end of every word.

**2** **Sling your own slang:** Accents aren't the only way people speak differently in different areas. They can use different names for the same thing, such as "pop" or "soda" for carbonated soft drinks. The place where you put luggage in a car is a trunk in the United States and a boot in England. If someone from Australia asks you, "Fair dinkum?" they want to know if you're telling the truth. Make up your own words or sayings and you've got the start of a separate language.

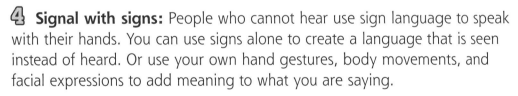

Do you like ice CREAM?

**3** **Play around with your own sounds:** Along with different words, you can try using a different set of sounds. Some languages use sounds that are not used in English. For example, some African languages use clicking noises made with the tongue the same way we use vowels and consonants to form words. Or try making your voice go up or down while you speak. When Americans ask a question, their voices go up at the end of a sentence. Try saying, "You like cookies. Do you like ice cream?" to hear the different **inflections**. In China, making your voice go up or down actually changes the entire meaning of the word. So the same word can mean pear, plum, or chestnut, depending on the tone you use.

**4** **Signal with signs:** People who cannot hear use sign language to speak with their hands. You can use signs alone to create a language that is seen instead of heard. Or use your own hand gestures, body movements, and facial expressions to add meaning to what you are saying.

**5** **Substitute your own alphabet:** The micronation of Molossia uses an abandoned alphabet that was invented by Mormons in Utah. An alphabet is just a code, and you can develop your own to write messages that only citizens of your country can read. To create your own version of the Latin alphabet used for most European languages, just write out the 26 letters from A to Z. Then, underneath each letter, put down the symbols for your new alphabet. Make sure everyone in your country has a copy of the new alphabet so you can send messages back and forth.

# COMPOSE YOUR OWN
## National Anthem

The national anthem of a country is a song that expresses the citizens' love for their country. Your national anthem is a song your citizens can sing on important occasions. You can make up your own words and music. Or do what many countries have done and change the words to a song you already know. The tune of the American national anthem, "The Star Spangled Banner," originally went to an old English song. Another patriotic American song, "My Country, 'Tis of Thee," is sung to the tune of the British national anthem, "God Save the Queen."

**1** Jot down some things that make you proud about your micronation.

**2** Find a melody that matches the mood and write lyrics that fit. If you create a web site for your micronation, you can post a video of you singing your original national anthem.

## Micronational Anthems

The Aerican national anthem was adopted in 2012 at the micronation's 25th anniversary celebration. Its second verse is:

*I have seen the penguins marching*　　*All hail!*
*To all of the world's ends;*　　*All hail the Aerican Empire!*
*If home is where I hang my towel,*　　*All hail! All hail!*
*it's better with friends!*　　*Within certain reasonable limits!*
*I've visited different lands*　　*Home is where I hang my towel!*
*I've seen cultures worldwide*　　*Home is where I hang my towel!*
*I'll choose to hang up my towel*　　*I love the Empire, for home is*
*In the Empire with pride!*　　*where I hang my towel!*

The French micronation of Le Saugeais has a national anthem that goes:

*We take great pride in Le Saugeais,*
*It's a fire no one can quench,*
*In fact we're a little bit prouder,*
*Than if we were just French.*

# CHAPTER SEVEN

## Your Country and the World

**NO COUNTRY CAN EXIST ON ITS OWN.**
Real countries interact in many ways. They exchange
representatives. They form **alliances** and organizations. They
hold international shows and competitions. They go to war
and they sign peace treaties. And they work together on
building projects and technology that can help the entire world.
The same is true for micronations. Both real countries and
micronations must pay attention to what is happening outside
their borders if they want to help their citizens lead happy lives.

# International Competition and Cooperation

Two main things cause countries to compete or cooperate—land and resources. When countries can't agree on where the border between them is located or when they decide they want resources that belong to another country, war can break out. But if they're willing to **negotiate**, they may be able to find a way to satisfy both sides.

*Diplomats are government officials who represent their country in talks with other countries.*

A country may also send an **ambassador** to another country to set up a permanent **embassy**. Diplomats play an important role in international affairs. In 1776, when the United States declared itself to be a separate country, one of the first things it did was send a diplomat to France. Because the job was so important, the new government sent Benjamin Franklin, one of the leaders of the American Revolution. Franklin convinced the French government to help the United States fight England. With France's help, America won the War of Independence.

## WORDS TO KNOW!

**alliance:** two or more allies joining up to work together.

**negotiate:** discussing something in order to reach an agreement about it.

**ambassador:** the head diplomat who represents the government of one country in dealings with another country or organization.

**embassy:** the office of an ambassador.

## FASCINATING FACT

PoliNation is an international meeting of micronations from around the world. The event takes place in different cities, including Perugia, Italy, in 2014 and in San Francisco in 2016.

Treaties lay out the details of agreements between countries on important topics. They can end arguments over where borders go. They can arrange trade between countries for goods and raw materials. Countries also sign treaties promising to defend their allies in case of attack. A peace treaty between two countries is an agreement to stop fighting with one another. Treaties are also made when a group of countries agrees to limit how much pollution countries release into the water or air they all must share.

But countries get together for less serious reasons, too. The Olympics is an international sports competition that is held every two years in a different country. And world fairs are exhibitions where countries can share their cultures and show off their industries.

## Join the United Nations

Several micronations have sent applications to the United Nations. So far, none has been successful in gaining membership. The aims of the United Nations are to help keep peace throughout the world, develop friendly relations between nations, work together to help people live better lives, protect the environment, and encourage respect for each other's rights and freedoms. If your country ever joins the United Nations, you will have to agree to treat other countries equally, try to settle differences peacefully, and avoid using threats or force.

# Interview with His Imperial Majesty Doctor Eric Lis of the Aerican Empire

Dr. Eric Lis of Montreal, Canada, created the Aerican Empire more than 25 years ago, and it is still going strong. Here he discusses inventing his own country.

**You created Aerica at the age of 5. What kinds of things did you learn in the course of building and maintaining it?**

I've learned a lot about how "real" governments run, both from reading about them and seeing what worked (and what failed spectacularly!) when I tried it. I've learned a great deal about different countries and nations around the world, and about some of the simple but profound ways they see the world differently from each other.

Most importantly, I've learned a lot of important lessons about myself: what my values are when I'm forced to explain and defend them, what I think is important enough to argue about and what isn't, what I want people to say about me when I'm not in the room, and what sort of world I want to live in.

**Can any kid create his or her own country? What does it take to be a micronational leader?**

Anyone can create a nation. It's easy! Creating a nation is as simple as looking around one day and deciding it exists. It's so easy, that some of the people reading this sentence will have already created one by the time they reach the period at the end. The hard part, and the most important part of being a micronational leader, is sticking with it. Creating a nation is a huge amount of fun!

Once it's created, though, you have to build it, expand it, develop it, and usually attract other people to join it, and these steps are less fun. Developing a rich and vibrant nation takes work. It gets boring. It can be repetitive. It can be worse than doing homework after school. But it needs doing, because everything worth building takes some hard work and frustration.

**When you were a kid, what was the best part of having your own country? What is the best part now?**

When I was a kid, the best part was feeling that I was different from the other kids. Sometimes more special, sometimes more powerful, often just weirder. As I've grown older—not grown "up" mind you, just older—the best part has become knowing that, through Aerica, I've had the chance to meet hundreds of people from all walks of life. I've contributed a little bit of silliness to countless lives and helped make the world a slightly stranger, more interesting place. I've made a positive impact on a lot of lives and I've made friends doing it. Who could ask for better than that? And the best part is, it shows no sign of stopping any time soon.

# HOST YOUR OWN
## Micronational World's Fair

Have you enjoyed inventing your own country? You've learned how geography and climate and landscape affect culture and economy and infrastructure. You've thought about what your country's theme and values are and what kinds of things are popular among your citizens. As you've gone through this book, you've created your country's symbols, learned how to write your own important documents, made stamps and money, and invented your own language. Now it's time to take your micronation out on the world stage.

A world's fair is a chance for countries to share their history and culture with people from other places. Usually, each country has its own building where it displays artifacts, works of art, and examples of new or interesting products. You can get together with friends who have their own micronations and hold your own world's fair. It also makes a great project for a school.

Let each micronational leader set up a display and talk about his or her country. You can also have performances or hold games. Have fun and learn about other micronations!

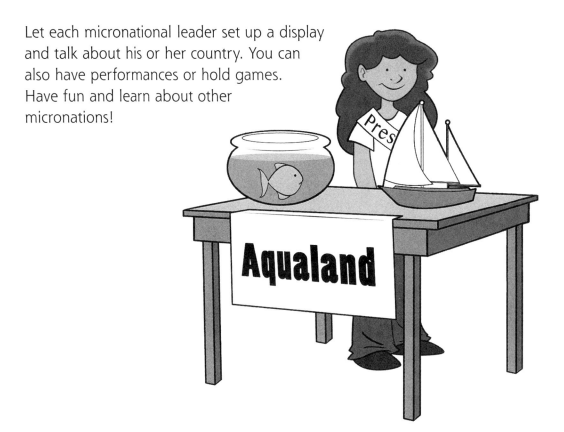

# CREATE YOUR OWN
# Atlas of Your Favorite Micronations

An atlas is a book with information about different places. If you take a look at a world atlas, you'll probably see the same format on each page: a map of the country, images of the country and its symbols, a short description, and a list of categories of information about the country.

You can create an atlas of micronations the same way. They can be countries run by your friends or micronations you read about online or in books. If your school hosted a micronational world's fair, your school can put together the world atlas of all its micronations. Include photographs or drawings of each country's flag, coat of arms, stamps, money, and symbols of authority.
**Here are some other kinds of information you can include:**

* Name of Country
* Theme, Description, or History
* Name and Title of Leader
* Names and Titles of Other Officials
* Type of Government
* Capital City
* Size
* Location
* Geography
* Population
* Climate

* Natural Resources
* Main Industries and Exports
* Language
* System of Measurement
* Popular Culture, including food, sports, entertainment, music

# GLOSSARY

**accent:** a particular way of saying words, usually used by people from one area.

**alliance:** two or more allies joining up to work together.

**ally:** a country that agrees to help and support another country.

**ambassador:** the head diplomat who represents the government of one country in dealings with another country or organization.

**amend:** to change a law.

**anesthesia:** medicine used during an operation to put patients to sleep and keep them from feeling pain.

**apprentice:** a person who learns a job or skill by working for someone who is good at it.

**aqueduct:** a network of channels used to direct water over long distances from its source to where it will be used.

**archipelago:** a group of islands, usually arranged in a line near a bigger piece of land.

**Arctic Circle:** a line of latitude near the North Pole.

**artifact:** an object made by humans.

**atlas:** a book with maps and information about different places.

**atmosphere:** the blanket of air surrounding the earth.

**axis:** the imaginary stick that the earth rotates around.

**barter:** to trade by exchanging one good or service for another.

**BCE:** put after a date, BCE stands for Before Common Era and counts down to zero. CE stands for Common Era and counts up from zero. These non-religious terms correspond to BC and AD.

**bill of rights:** a document that spells out some of the rights that belong to the citizens of a country.

**candidate:** a person who runs for an office in the government.

**capital:** the city where the government of a state or country is based.

**capitalist:** a free market system.

**cartography:** the art and science of making maps.

**censor:** when the government blocks citizens from seeing certain information.

**characteristic:** a feature of a person, place, or thing.

**citizen:** a person who legally belongs to a country and has the rights and protection of that country.

**civil war:** a war between groups of people in the same country.

**clan:** a large group of related families.

**climate:** the average weather in an area during a long period of time.

**climate change:** changes in the earth's climate patterns, including rising temperatures, which is called global warming.

**coat of arms:** a design made of several symbols that represents a family or country.

**cobbler:** a person who makes shoes.

**co-exist:** to live in peace with each other.

**colony:** an area that is controlled by or belongs to another country.

**command economy:** a system in which everything belongs to the government, which decides what is made and how much it costs.

**communication:** methods of sending information.

**communist:** a system in which everything is owned and run by the government.

**community currency:** money that can only be used in the community that created it.

**compass rose:** a circle drawn on a map to show north, south, east, and west.

# GLOSSARY

**competition:** trying to get something another person or company wants at the same time.

**compromise:** an agreement reached by two sides working together.

**conflict:** a long period of disagreement that sometimes includes violence.

**consonant:** sounds made by letters that are not vowels (a, e, i, o, and u).

**constitution:** a document that describes a country's rules and laws and how its government is set up.

**consumer:** a person who buys goods and services.

**continent:** one of the earth's large landmasses, including Africa, Antarctica, Australia, North America, South America, and Asia and Europe (called Eurasia).

**coordinates:** a set of numbers or directions that tell you where a place is.

**coronation:** a ceremony to crown a monarch.

**counterfeit:** a fake version.

**country:** a place with official boundaries, called borders, that mark it off from other places. A country can make agreements or fight wars with other countries.

**crop:** a plant grown for food and other uses.

**cuisine:** food that is cooked in a particular way or food that a country is known for.

**cultural geography:** the way people interact with their surroundings. Also called human geography.

**culture:** the beliefs and way of life of a group of people, which can include religion, language, art, clothing, food, holidays, and more.

**currency:** money.

**current:** the steady flow of water or air in one direction.

**data:** information in the form of facts and numbers.

**declaration of independence:** an announcement to the world that a new country has formed. The U.S. Declaration of Independence was written in 1776 to explain why America was separating itself from Britain and becoming its own country.

**democracy:** a government where citizens pick the leaders and have a say in how things are run.

**dialect:** a form of a language used by people in one area.

**dictator:** a ruler with unlimited control whose power comes from the military.

**dimension:** the size of something given as a measurement, such as "1 foot high."

**diplomat:** a person sent by the government to deal with another country.

**draft:** an early version of a document that still needs more work.

**earthquake:** a sudden movement of the earth's crust caused by tectonic plates slipping along a fault.

**economy:** the system of making and exchanging things of value.

**elect:** to choose someone by vote.

**election:** a vote where citizens get to choose a leader.

**elevation:** height above sea level.

**embassy:** the office of an ambassador.

**employer:** a person or company that hires people to work for pay.

**enforce:** to carry out a law.

**equator:** an imaginary line drawn around the middle of the earth. The line forms a circle halfway between the North and South poles.

**eruption:** a violent explosion of gas, steam, or ash.

# GLOSSARY

**exchange rate:** the value of one country's money in terms of another country's money.

**executive:** the branch of government that includes the leader and the advisors who run the country.

**export:** any good or service that is shipped outside the country or brings in money from other countries.

**fault:** where two tectonic plates meet.

**federal:** national, covering the whole country.

**fee:** the cost of doing something.

**fertile:** describes soil that is good for growing crops.

**fraternity:** brotherhood or connection to fellow human beings.

**free market economy:** a system where people are free to buy and sell things they own.

**freedom of religion:** a person's right to practice his or her religion without interference from the government.

**freedom of the press:** the right to publish news stories without interference from the government.

**geography:** the study of the earth and its features, such as mountains and rivers, and the effect of human activity on the earth.

**geology:** the scientific study of the history and physical nature of the earth.

**GIS:** Geographic Information System, a type of computer program used for making maps that can show different kinds of information.

**goods:** things that are made or grown.

**government:** an organization or system that controls a city, state, or country.

**government in exile:** a government that tries to keep running after it has been forced out of the country.

**GPS:** Global Positioning System, a system of satellites, computers, and receivers that can determine the exact location of a receiver anywhere on the planet.

**homeschool:** to teach children at home, usually done by the parents.

**House of Representatives:** the legislative body in the United States that has representatives from 435 districts across the country. Each district has roughly the same population. Some states have more districts than others.

**Ice Age:** a period of time when ice covers a large part of the earth.

**identity:** the unique characteristics of a person, country, or group.

**import:** any good or service that is brought in from another country.

**inflection:** a rise or fall in the sound of a person's voice.

**infrastructure:** roads, bridges, and other basic types of structures and equipment needed for a country to function properly.

**invasion:** when one country or group moves in to take over another country.

**irrigation:** a system of ditches to transport water through farmland.

**judicial:** the branch of government consisting of courts with judges who decide if laws have been broken.

**key:** a chart that explains all the symbols used on a map.

**landform:** a natural feature of the earth's surface, such as a mountain or river.

**landmark:** a natural or man-made object that is easy to see and recognize.

**latitude:** an imaginary line that goes around the earth and runs parallel to the equator. It measures your position on earth north or south of the equator.

# GLOSSARY

**legislative:** the branch of government that makes the laws.

**liberty:** freedom, the ability to act or live freely as one chooses.

**license:** permission to do something.

**locavore:** a person who makes an effort to eat food that is grown close by.

**longitude:** imaginary lines running through the North and South poles that indicate where you are on the globe east or west of the Prime Meridian.

**loophole:** a mistake or unclear wording in a law that people use to avoid following the law exactly.

**mace:** a ceremonial stick carried by an official as a sign of authority in a legislature.

**magma:** hot liquid rock below the surface of the earth.

**majority:** most of the people or voters.

**map:** a picture or diagram of the earth's surface.

**mass transit:** a system for moving large numbers of people on buses, trains, or other vehicles.

**media:** the industry in the business of presenting news to the public, by methods including radio, television, Internet, and newspapers.

**merchant:** someone who buys and sells goods for profit.

**metric system:** a system of weights and measures based on the number 10.

**micronation:** an imaginary country that has many features of a real country, but is not considered real by other countries.

**microstate:** a real nation that is extremely small.

**military:** the army, navy, air force, and other armed services that protect a country and fight in wars.

**minerals:** naturally occurring solids found in rocks and in the ground. Rocks are made of minerals. Gold and diamonds are precious minerals.

**minority:** the side with fewer supporters.

**molten:** melted into liquid by heat.

**monetary system:** a country's laws and systems for controlling how money is made and used, including mints to print more money and banks to distribute it.

**monopoly:** when there is only one supplier or group of suppliers for a good or service.

**motto:** a saying that represents the main belief or purpose of a person, group, or country.

**mythology:** a collection of traditional stories, either truthful or overly elaborated, that are often focused on historical events. Myths express the beliefs and values of a group of people.

**national anthem:** a song played as a mark of loyalty to the nation.

**nation:** another word for country, also used to refer to a group of people who share a common culture even if they don't live in their own country.

**natural resource:** something from nature that people can use in some way, such as water, stone, and wood.

**naturalize:** to make someone a citizen.

**negotiate:** discussing something in order to reach an agreement about it.

**nonprofit:** an organization supported by donations whose main mission is to help people, animals, the environment, or other causes.

**nonrenewable:** not able to be replaced.

**passport:** a document from the government that identifies a person as a citizen of the country.

**patriotic:** showing love for your country.

**119**

# GLOSSARY

**patron saint:** a person from history, legend, or religious tradition who is looked up to as a hero or protector for a particular group of people.

**physical geography:** the land, water, and weather in an area.

**pidgin:** a simple form of a language used to help people who speak different languages do business together.

**Pig Latin:** a play language formed by moving the sounds around in words.

**pole:** the points at the top and bottom of the globe where an imaginary stick, or axis, would stick out.

**political:** relating to running a government and holding onto power.

**political party:** a group that holds particular ideas about how to run the government.

**population:** the number of people living in a place.

**preamble:** an introduction to a document that states the reasons for creating it.

**printing press:** a machine that prints multiple copies of a document.

**profit:** the amount gained by transferring something of value to someone else for more than it cost.

**province:** a particular part that a country is divided into.

**public health:** a system that works to keep the population as a whole healthy.

**raw material:** something used to make something else. Natural resources are raw materials.

**recognize:** to officially accept something as being true.

**regulate:** to control something with laws and supervision.

**remote sensing:** measuring the features of the earth over long distances with cameras and other tools.

**renewable resource:** a resource that nature can replace.

**repeal:** to cancel a law.

**reservoir:** a man-made or natural lake used to store water for drinking and other uses.

**resident:** a person who lives in a place permanently or for a long time.

**revenue:** money coming in.

**revolt:** to fight against a government or person of authority.

**revolution:** when the people overthrow the government.

**rotation:** a turn all the way around.

**royal:** having to do with a king or queen.

**satellite:** a spacecraft that permanently circles the earth high above its surface to send and receive TV, cell phone, and other communications signals.

**scale:** the size of a map, model, drawing, or diagram compared to the actual object, shown as two measurements in relation to one another, such as "1 inch to 3 miles" or 1:3.

**scepter:** a ceremonial stick carried by a monarch as a sign of authority.

**sea level:** the level of the surface of the sea.

**seal:** an official symbol that shows that a document or other object belongs to the government.

**secede:** to break away from a country.

**Senate:** the legislative body in the United States that has two representatives for every state.

**services:** jobs and businesses that provide something for other people but do not produce goods.

**Silk Road:** the ancient network of trade routes connecting the Mediterranean Sea and China by land.

**socialist:** combining capitalist and communist methods. The government provides services but private property is allowed.

# GLOSSARY

**soil:** the top layer of the earth.

**solar power:** electricity created by special panels that convert the energy of the sun.

**species:** a group of plants or animals that are closely related and look the same.

**statehood:** the existence of an independent state or country.

**status:** the position of someone in a group.

**supply and demand:** the rule that prices go up and down depending on how much there is of something and how much people want it.

**Supreme Court:** the highest court of law in a country, with the top panel of judges.

**surveying tools:** special instruments for taking measurements over long distances.

**symbolic:** something that is important because of what it stands for or represents.

**tax:** money collected by the government to help it run.

**tectonic plate:** a large section of the earth's crust that moves on top of the hot melted layer below.

**telegraph:** a device for tapping out coded messages over wires using electrical signals.

**theme:** a central, recurring idea or concept.

**three-dimensional (3-D):** an image that has length, width, and height, and is raised off the flat page.

**time zone:** a region where all clocks are set to the same time. There are 24 time zones, each one an hour ahead of the zone to the west.

**trade:** the buying, selling, or exchange of goods and services between countries.

**tradition:** a custom or belief that has been handed down in a community or culture over many years.

**traditional economy:** a system where a group of people all work together and almost everything belongs to the group.

**transportation:** methods of travel.

**treaty:** a written agreement between two countries.

**tribe:** a group of clans with the same language, customs, and beliefs.

**turnpike:** a major road that you pay to use.

**tutor:** a teacher who works with only one student, often privately in the student's home.

**ultraviolet light:** a type of light that cannot be seen by human eyes.

**union:** a group that represents workers when dealing with the employer.

**Union Jack:** the national flag of Great Britain, showing red and white crossed stripes on a blue background.

**United Nations (UN):** an organization of countries started in 1945 to encourage peace and improve living conditions around the world. It is based in New York City. Today the UN has 193 member countries.

**vaccine:** medicine designed to keep a person from getting a particular disease, usually given by needle.

**value:** how much money something is worth.

**volcano:** a mountain formed by magma or ash forcing its way from deep inside the earth to the surface.

**vowel:** the sounds made by the letters a, e, i, o, and u.

**wealth:** money and valuable belongings.

**wind power:** electricity created by windmills turned by the wind.

**work force:** all the workers.

**world-building:** the process of inventing an imaginary world in a book, movie, or game.

# RESOURCES

## Books

*How Governments Work: The Inside Guide to the Politics of the World*, DK Adult, 2006

*The Kingfisher Geography Encyclopedia* by Clive Gifford, Kingfisher, 2003

*Don't Know Much About Geography* by Kenneth C. Davis, Harper Paperbacks, 2013

*The Prentice Hall Atlas of World History*, Pearson, 2008

*National Geographic World Atlas For Young Explorers*, National Geographic Children's Books, 2007

*Economy* by Johnny Acton and David Goldblatt, DK Eyewitness Books, 2010

*What the World Eats* by Faith D'Aluisio and Peter Menzel, Tricycle Press, 2008

*A Life Like Mine: How Children Live Around the World*, DK Publishing, 2002

*Children Just Like Me* by Barnabas and Anabel Kindersley, DK Children, 1995

*Micronations: The Lonely Planet Guide to Home-Made Nations* by John Ryan, Lonely Planet, 2006

*How to Build Your Own Country* by Valerie Wyatt and Fred Rix, Kids Can Press, 2009

## Web Sites

**Constitutions of the World in English**
www.constitution.org/cons/natlcons.htm

**CIA World Factbook**
www.cia.gov/cia/publications/factbook/index.html

**Council on Foreign Relations** www.cfr.org

**Republic of Molossia** www.molossia.org

**How to Start Your Own Micronation by Kevin Baugh of Molossia**
micronations.webs.com

**The Aerican Empire** www.aericanempire.com

**Micronation Central** www.listofmicronations.com

**PoliNation** www.micronationconference.com

# INDEX

**123**

# INDEX